Southern cultures

Spring 2003
Published by the
University of North Carolina Press
for the
Center for the Study of the American South
at the University of North Carolina at Chapel Hill

Letters to the Editors Britney's Ghost, *1*

"*I figured I'd better wait awhile to see if y'all would settle down and get back to doing what you do best: aggravating people, but not insulting them.*"

Front Porch, *4*

by Harry L. Watson

"*If you've never thought of yin and yang as southern* ⋯⋯⋯⋯"

Essays

D1535572

Our Kind of Yankee, *9*

by John Shelton Reed

"*What's going on here? Texans and South Carolinians playing kissy-face with New York City? Isn't New York the heart of Yankeedom? Isn't it the city southerners love to hate?*"

Yankee Interloper and Native Son: Carl Carmer and Clarence Cason, *18*

By Philip Beidler

"'*Like a fickle lover, the South has a way of tormenting those who care most about her.*'"

In Search of the Lost Confederate Graveyard, *36*

photographs by Charlie Curtis

"*At last Curtis could sense that he was closing in on the lost Confederates.*"

Heritage, not Hate? Collecting Black Memorabilia, *43*

by Lynn Casmier-Paz

"*When I arrived at the Silver Spring Armory, I found the place jammed with brown and black people hawking rusted 'Authentic Slave Shackles' that only a consumer with a platinum credit card could purchase.*"

My Twentieth Century: Leaves from a Journal, *62*

by Anne Firor Scott

"*For a moment the world stopped turning while we, a great nation, felt ourselves suddenly headless, directionless.*"

Mason-Dixon Lines Audubon Drive, Memphis, *79*
poetry by Jim Seay
"Elvis is about twenty-one and 'Heartbreak Hotel' has just sold a million."

Up Beat Down South "The Death of Emma Hartsell," *82*
by Bruce E. Baker
*"One December afternoon, he finished off a running argument
with his younger brother-in-law with both barrels of a shotgun."*

Books

Harlan Greene
Mr. Skylark: John Bennett and the Charleston Renaissance, *92*
reviewed by Dale Volberg Reed
*"Charleston society cut him dead, and he began again
the cycle of illness, depression, and addiction.*

Harvey Broome
Out Under the Sky of the Great Smokies: A Personal Journal, *96*
reviewed by Daniel S. Pierce
*"Broome relished hiking through mist-shrouded old-growth forests,
sleeping in the rain, or rock-hopping in winter on ice-covered boulders."*

Michelle Brattain
The Politics of Whiteness: Race, Workers, and Culture in the Modern South, *98*
reviewed by Carl Burkart
*"No wonder federal efforts to integrate schools and workplaces
met with hard-line opposition from white mill-hands."*

Carol K. Bleser and Lesley J. Gordon, Editors
Intimate Strategies of the Civil War: Military Commanders and Their Wives, *100*
reviewed by Nina Silber
*"Would the war have gone differently if Stonewall Jackson
or William Sherman had listened more to their wives?"*

Don H. Doyle
Faulkner's County: The Historical Roots of Yoknapatawpha, *102*
reviewed by Linda Wagner-Martin
"Faulkner and his work remain lynchpins of the study of southern culture."

Benjamin R. Justesen
George Henry White: An Even Chance in the Race of Life, *104*
    reviewed by John H. Haley
    "In July 1900, George Henry White allegedly stated,
    'May God damn North Carolina, the state of my birth.'"

Randy J. Sparks
Religion in Mississippi, *106*
    reviewed by David Edwin Harrell Jr.
    "'Attacked by right-wing segregationists for being too liberal and almost equally
    denounced by their coreligionists outside the region for being too conservative,
    white religious leaders across the state were virtually paralyzed.'"

About the Contributors, *109*

Britney's Ghost
More Fallout from Our Most Controversial Cover

It turns out that it would have been easier to quit the Mafia. We're referring to our attempt to place a little time and distance between our current work and the now-infamous Winter 2002 cover photo of a bare-bellied Britney Spears. Not that we mind entirely, of course. But since the pop diva's navel graced our pages—over a year ago—we've published essays and articles about re-fighting the Civil War, the songs of the South, Jackie Robinson's breakthrough into baseball, southern religions, the Confederate Flag controversy, the Neshoba County Fair, Robert E. Lee's inner battles, the Father of the Blues and the search for his soul, the investigation into a missing ghost ship's crew, the dying art of deer-driving, and many, many other topics. And what do our readers have to say about all this? Well, not nearly as much as they have to say about Britney. If she's on your minds, though, she's on ours, too.

Of course, occasionally we do receive other types of complaints. Leonard Wilson, for instance, takes us to task for the tenor of our special *Biography* issue, and Michael Sabota objects to us on general grounds and even declares us guilty by affiliation. We begin and end, though, with two letters from Alma M. Womack. The first is a saucy rant about you-know-who, *that* cover, and our proper place (which, it turns out, is not in the music business). Then, in the last of this issue's letters, Ms. Womack follows up on her earlier correspondence—and, it seems, she even forgives us.

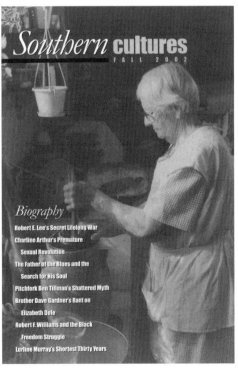

The offending and redeeming covers, according to long-time reader Alma M. Womack.

I was all set to order two gift subscriptions for Christmas presents for a couple of my friends. They had been assured that *Southern Cultures* was a worthwhile read, considering that most of your contributors are too liberal to get along with regular people. Then I got the issue with Britney Spears on the cover. I could not, in good conscience, order a publication for my friends with a half nekkid kid on the front, and tell them that, hey, this is a literary magazine.

I figured I'd better wait awhile to see if y'all would settle down and get back to doing what you do best: aggravating people, but not insulting them. The current issue is much better, and I hope that your foray into the pop world is over. *Rolling Stone* can handle Britney better than you.

By the way, Britney Spears and her pageant mother just lived in Louisiana for a while. They no more represent our state than they do North Carolina, and they for darn sure don't represent southern girls and women.

Keep the aggravation flowing.

Alma M. Womack
Jonesville, Louisiana

Your Fall 2002 *Biography* issue defies a nomenclature like *Southern Cultures*. In this issue your Yankee writers denigrate great southerners like Robert E. Lee and Ben Tillman, while glorifying a criminal like Robert Williams. It is my suggestion that you find some qualified southern writers who can expound on topics relating to southern culture—instead of politically correct Yankees who are still trying to rewrite history.

More Lea Barton type articles ("Paradox in Paradise") would enhance your mission.

Leonard Wilson
Townley, Alabama

Since the infamous Britney cover appeared, Southern Cultures *has continued to publish essays and articles about a wide variety of topics, including "Through the Cumberland Gap" from our special* After a Confederate Childhood *issue, in which Doris Betts asked, "Who ever aspired to be Dale Evans?" Photograph courtesy of the Museum of Modern Art Film Stills Archive. All Rights Reserved.*

I am canceling my subscription for two reasons. First, as a white southern male I am offended by some of the articles that you have published. The other reason is your university's efforts to make incoming freshmen read excerpts from The Koran. It is sad that a southern institution has lost touch with what it means to be southern and American. I want a refund as I do not want one cent of my money to support your "university" in any way. I hope real southerners and Americans boycott your school. You are an embarrassment to your state and the South in general. Goodbye.

Michael Sabota
(via email)

Previously, I wrote a letter to you, chastising you for putting Britney Spears on the cover of your magazine. After receiving the Fall 2002 *Biography* issue, I want to tell you that you are forgiven for your earlier mishap.

The cover picture and story inside about the forgotten farmwomen of the South was just excellent ("'God Giveth the Increase': Lurline Stokes Murray's Narrative of Farming and Faith"). Mrs. Murray could be all of our grandmothers and great grandmothers who kept the family strong and the farm going in the difficult times that they lived in. I could just see my own womenfolk of the past in Lu Ann Jones's article, and I appreciate so much the time and research that she put into her study of these forgotten rural women. I ordered the book by Ms. Jones, *Mama Learned Us to Work*, so that I could read all that she had to say about Mrs. Murray and the other women of her time who learned us all.

Overall, the *Biography* issue was one of your best yet, and I am glad that I didn't "runn oft" after the Britney cover disappointed me so. Thank you again for the wonderful story on real Southern women.

A satisfied customer,
Alma M. Womack

Ed. note: Email SouthernCultures@unc.edu *or send your correspondence to: Letters to the Editors,* Southern Cultures, *CB#9127, UNC-CH, Chapel Hill, NC 27599-9127. We'll assume letters received at this address or by email are intended for publication, subject to editing. If we use your letter, we'll send you a free extra copy of the issue in which it appears.*

front porch

There used to be a kind of rag doll you could find in playrooms and on display in the homes of whimsical southern collectors. The one I remember clearest belonged to the only female doctor I knew and sat on a kitchen shelf beside the cookbooks. At first glance (depending on the owner's mood, that is) it appeared to depict a conventional white maiden with blond braids, a muslin frock, and a rosebud simper that gave no hint of mystery. But if you peered beneath her hems, a prying child would find an upside down torso, with head and arms where the feet should be. If you flipped the skirt entirely over the white doll's head, a black doll emerged, clad in an equally conventional head wrap, apron, and gingham work dress. Some versions gave a purse or bouquet to the white doll and a wooden spoon to her black counterpart, underscoring the social roles of each. Together, the two represented maid and mistress, literally joined at the hip.

above: *In "My Twentieth Century," preeminent historian Anne Firor Scott celebrates her eightieth birthday by looking back on the South, the country, and her place in the world as she has considered it through six decades of journal writing. The historian with her brother, David, in 1927, courtesy of Anne Firor Scott.*

These dolls would probably fit comfortably into one of the Black Memorabilia Showcases stocked with "grotesque" images and figurines described by Lynn Casmier-Paz in her article, "Heritage, not Hate? Collecting Black Memorabilia." Memory may be playing tricks, but the ones I remember were not necessarily grotesque, just simple and straightforward, as rag dolls tend to be. The joke lay in representing African American and white women as mirror images of each other, despite the chasms of difference we were supposed to feel between them. Looking at the dolls, the ironic stereotypes came forward with a rush, each the flip side of the other. Mammy and Scarlett, housemaid and debutante, hussy and ice queen, the dolls seemed to say, all were sisters beneath the skin. Or skirt. As Mary Boykin Chesnut used to say, "There is no slave like a wife."

Of all these paired opposites, I suspect it was the combination of professional and homemaker that most closely touched the life of my 1950s neighbor, as she flipped her skirt back and forth to change herself from family slave to medical doctor and back again, each on a daily basis. But this being the South, the closeness and distance of white and African American had been a cultural reality for centuries, and toys like hers, I suspect, had been around southern dollhouses for quite a while.

Paired opposites appear with frequency in this issue of *Southern Cultures*. Our coeditor John Shelton Reed opens up with some reflections on New York City, once the avatar of everything old-fashioned southerners claimed to hate about the North. In the aftermath of September 11, Reed observes, southerners seemed to have reversed field, to remember what they find heroic about ordinary New Yorkers, who emerged from the horrors of that day displaying the kind of elemental courage and dignity that diehard Rebels profess to admire even more than the rest of us. Like the rag doll, he tells us, North and South may be polar opposites but they are also sisters under the skin.

Carl Carmer and Clarence Cason were twins of another kind, Philip Beidler finds. Both were professors at the University of Alabama in the 1930s, both wrote critical books about the state, and both scored similar points against its prevailing culture. But literary Alabama reviled Carmer as a sniping carpetbagger who betrayed his hosts, while Cason the native son found forgiveness when he did what seemed to be the honorable thing and committed suicide a few days before his unsparing book came out. W. J. Cash, North Carolina's more famous counterpart to the Alabama twins, met a similar end when his blockbuster analysis *The Mind of the South* appeared a few years later. Carmer and Cason, carpetbagger and scalawag, Beidler explains, said similar things but met opposite fates, both reflecting the region's apparent inability to tolerate the contradictions embodied in a loving criticism. Ironically, Carmer's title, *Stars Fell on Alabama*, now appears as a slogan on state license plates in the space where "The Heart of Dixie" used to be. In the New Alabama of skyscrapers and Mercedes plants, it seems, the Old

In "Our Kind of Yankee," John Shelton Reed says that one thing southerners have always disliked about northerners is their stereotypical view of a Deliverance *kind of South. From* Deliverance, *courtesy of the Museum of Modern Art Film Stills Archive. Copyright by Warner Brothers, Incorporated, 1972. All Rights Reserved.*

South overtones of the former slogan have given way to the image of blessings raining from on high. If Alabama is ready to forgive and forget, can the rest of Dixie be far behind?

Lynn Casmier-Paz explores the deeper meaning of paired opposites in her analysis of "black memorabilia." If the twinned black and white rag dolls I remember illustrate a linkage between what was honored and what was demeaned in the 1950s, Casmier-Paz explores the tie between what is desired and what is loathed in African American memory. Caricatured icons of white racism once abounded in the advertisements and souvenir shops of white America, depicting African Americans as degraded animals with inhuman features. Casmier-Paz reports that some affluent African Americans now avidly collect these "black memorabilia," paying high prices to treasure what was formerly loathsome. Defending this practice, prominent collectors like Julian Bond and Henry Louis Gates have claimed that when African Americans own these objects, their hurtful power diminishes and purchasers acquire a proud totem of their victory over the forces

Charlie Curtis goes "In Search of a Lost Confederate Graveyard" and encounters a Virginian backwoods full of secrets, including these cattle remains. Photograph by Charlie Curtis.

that once oppressed them. In this view, the statuette of a grinning Sambo is not so much a genuine depiction of blackness as an illustration of the defeated adversary's mentality, and thus a very fitting trophy for the now-victorious African American collector.

Casmier-Paz is not so sure. To her, the abused African American children and grinning Sambos of bygone advertising and yard art are still hurtful, no matter who owns them. She wonders whether the hope of making money in the high-stakes collectibles market is driving some collectors to forget their history and worries that many African Americans are not as safe from the violence depicted in these materials as those who collect them. It's a touchy subject, and Julian Bond offers a sharp rejoinder to Casmier-Paz's accusations, in response to our invitation. In effect, the collectors feel that they can change the dolls' meaning by turning them upside down, as it were. Whatever your own view, this exercise only reminds me of how close to each other the honored and the demeaned can be, and once more, how each can hide beneath the skirts of the other.

There's not much that's ambivalent about Anne Firor Scott's memoir of her career as one of the first professional historians of women in the modern South. "My Twentieth Century: Leaves from a Journal" draws on her voluminous private writings and describes her journey from 1930s Athens, Georgia, not far in space or spirit from the Tuscaloosa of Carmer and Cason, to the academic heights of Duke and Radcliffe. Scott's famous first book also traced a journey: *The Southern Lady: From Pedestal to Politics*. Her recollections, offered on the occasion of her eightieth birthday, describe the journey from innocence to experience that likewise stresses how close the two can be. Certainly if all the rest of us could retain Scott's wit, grace, and gentility of spirit while gaining her wisdom and experience, the union of opposites would not seem so challenging.

In our "Up Beat Down South," Bruce Baker explores two lynching ballads, both composed within a few years of each other, both from the same region of North Carolina, and both sung to the same tune. One ballad praises the lynching of a suspected African American murderer; the other condemns a similar crime committed against a white man. The "black" song survived long enough to be recorded by a local string band; the "white" one is all but forgotten. Even so, the values of the critical ballad prevailed, for the crime of lynching is now virtually extinct where it once was chillingly commonplace. Far from finding the South solid on this question, Baker once more describes how opposites can keep close company in popular folkways, suggesting that ambivalence is closer to the center of southern culture than critics like W. J. Cash have suggested.

Two aesthetic pieces round out our issue: a photographic essay by Charlie Curtis and an Elvis poem by James Seay. Both dwell on death and life, past and expectancy, and maybe a little on black and white. If you've never thought of yin and yang as southern symbols, maybe you will now. And if you don't, perhaps a reversible rag doll will seem more like it.

HARRY L. WATSON, *Coeditor*

Our Kind of Yankee

September 11 Reminded Southerners of What We Admire about New York

by John Shelton Reed

These are the kind of New Yorkers we saw on television after September 11: firemen, policemen, rescue workers—ordinary folks. They're our kind of Yankee. Photograph by Tom Sperduto, courtesy of the U.S. Coast Guard.

n the days after September 11, when Americans were watching a lot of television, many of us heard a Texas man-in-the-street tell a network interviewer something like, "Being a Texan or New Yorker just isn't very important right now. We're all Americans." Soon after that, we heard about some South Carolina middle-school students who raised the money to buy a truck for some Brooklyn firemen who lost theirs (along with seven comrades) at the World Trade Center.

What's going on here? Texans and South Carolinians playing kissy-face with New York City? Isn't New York the heart of Yankeedom? Isn't it the city southerners love to hate? Well, like other Americans in that great red Republican interior on the 2000 Presidential election map, many southerners do think at least occasionally of New York City as the Great Wen, the cesspool of iniquity, home of everything alien and vile. It has been suggested, not entirely in jest, that the city's evolution vindicates the Confederacy.

The bill of particulars has several components. First of all, there's a lot for everybody to dislike about New York: the welfare culture, deranged street people, dysfunctional public schools, periodic brushes with bankruptcy, wack-job politicians. Even many New Yorkers complain about this stuff, often while taking a perverse sort of pride in being able to cope with it.

But southerners have had some special reasons to dislike New York, starting with the fact that it is simply the most urban corner of America. A good many southerners have seen city life as bad for both morals and manners. When Thomas Jefferson celebrated individual ownership of land and the farming life as the only sound bases for culture and society, he was writing in what was already an old southern tradition. The most eloquent statement of the southern case against big cities probably came in 1930, with a manifesto by twelve southern men of letters called *I'll Take My Stand: The South and the Agrarian Tradition*. More recently, Hank Williams Jr. has often put the sentiment to music: in "Dixie on My Mind," for example, he complains, "These people never smile or say a word / They're all too busy trying to make an extra dime."

In addition, although this may be changing, many southerners have also taken a dim view of New York for serving as the great reception center and repository for foreign immigration. Our chambers of commerce, after all, used to brag about our "native born" labor force, and former Atlanta Brave John Rocker of Macon, Georgia, is not the only southern boy who thinks Americans ought to speak English. In general, ever since New York displaced Boston as the home of the ultra-Yankee, southerners have tended to see whatever we dislike about northerners as concentrated there. When we describe ourselves to pollsters as friendly, polite, hospitable, leisurely, traditional, conservative—well, it goes without saying who is not that way.

And what many of us really dislike about northerners, and thus loathe in spades

Soon after September 11, we heard about some South Carolina middle-school students who raised money to buy a truck for some Brooklyn firemen who lost theirs (along with seven comrades) at the World Trade Center. Photograph by Tom Sperduto, courtesy of the U.S. Coast Guard.

about New Yorkers, is their view of southerners as yokels—if not as *Deliverance*-style Neanderthals. Wherever northerners got their ideas of the South (and of course a southerner wrote *Deliverance*), some of them have indeed been inclined to view us as a lesser breed. Consider Kirkpatrick Sale's scare-mongering 1975 book, *Power Shift: The Rise of the Southern Rim and Its Challenge to the Eastern Establishment*, which extrapolated from economic and demographic trends to project the sort of nightmare future in which Mr. Sale's northeastern readers would have to choose between, say, a governor of Texas and a former senator from Tennessee for president. (One of the few pleasures of the 1992 Democratic convention for this southerner was watching the expression on Mario Cuomo's face every time he said the word "Arkansas.") I could go on, but the point is that there has been no love lost, in either direction, between New York City and the South. And in this, the South has merely been a 100-proof stand-in for places like Iowa,

Before September 11, even Tom Wolfe, who pretty well peeled, cored, and sliced the Big Apple in Bonfire of the Vanities, *once confessed, "I still find New York exciting, to tell the truth. It's not the easiest way to live in the world, but I still get a kick out of riding down Park Avenue in a cab at 2:30 in the morning and seeing the glass buildings all around." Photograph by Tom Sperduto, courtesy of the U.S. Coast Guard.*

Idaho, Ohio, and many other parts of what some New Yorkers call "flyover country." We all know this, don't we?

But, of course, it hasn't been quite that simple. Southerners, like other American heartlanders, have always been of two minds about the city. Some have looked on New York and New Yorkers with admiration, occasionally envy. Most of us can find at least something to admire about the place and its people.

For decades, of course, New York looked pretty good to black southerners. In the first half of the twentieth century, hundreds of thousands, especially from Georgia and the Carolinas, packed their worldly goods and box lunches and rode the Chickenbone Special out of the Jim Crow South, following the drinking gourd to seek a better life in Harlem and Bedford-Stuyvesant.

Many whites joined this exodus, especially a certain type of young southern intellectual for whom The City has always been where it's happening (whatever "it" may be). North Carolina's Thomas Wolfe set the pattern in the 1920s, and forty years later Mississippi's Willie Morris epitomized it. Morris's wince-making memoir, *New York Days*, is awash in isn't-it-wonderful-that-I'm-a-part-of-you-New-York-New-York gush. Even as confident and self-aware an expat as Tom Wolfe

New York City is part of the mental furniture of all Americans, and many of us think of the good things about New York as in some sense ours. Photograph courtesy of NYC & Company, Incorporated.

the younger, the Virginian who pretty well peeled, cored, and sliced the Big Apple in *Bonfire of the Vanities*, once confessed, "I still find New York exciting, to tell the truth. It's not the easiest way to live in the world, but I still get a terrific kick out of riding down Park Avenue in a cab at 2:30 in the morning and seeing the glass buildings all around. I have a real cornball attitude towards it, I suppose, which I think only somebody born far away from there would still have."

Southern writers and artists have historically had to look north to New York, because that's pretty much where the literary and artistic action was. Yet arty folk aren't the only ones who have feared, deep down, that nothing signifies unless it is noticed on that thin sliver of asphalt stretching between the Hudson and the East Rivers; plenty of hardheaded businesspeople feel the same. Atlanta, in particular, is full of the kind of strivers Tom Wolfe nailed in his 1998 novel, *A Man in Full*, for whom "the one thing they can't stand is the idea that somebody in New York might be calling them Southern hicks." (Houstonians, for some reason, don't have as bad a case of what the Australians call "cultural cringe": On the rare occasions when they think of New Yorkers at all, they're likely to feel sorry for them because they're not Texans.)

One might have thought that the South's astonishing economic development, the rise of southern cities, and the end of *de jure* segregation—all of which have made the South more like New York—would make New York City less alluring to some, and less repugnant to others. Increasingly, southerners don't have to leave home to find urban, cosmopolitan, polyglot settings. Now that we have our own street crime, pollution, and traffic problems, there should be less reason to feel superior. Now that we have our own opera companies and publishing houses and big-league sports, there would seem less reason to feel inferior. But we still think of New York as different, and, in some ways, special.

No matter where we grew up, few of us have entirely escaped the romance of The City. We know about the mean streets, sure, but we can't shake the image of Gene Kelly dancing in them. Thanks to *Mad* magazine and *The New Yorker*, to Irving Berlin and Hollywood, I knew about Coney Island and Harlem and the Upper East Side long before I ever set foot in New York. I recognized that socialites lived on Park Avenue, bums in the Bowery, bohemians in Greenwich Village. I understood who worked on Wall Street, and Madison Avenue, and Broadway, and in Tin Pan Alley.

New York City is part of the mental furniture of all Americans, and many of us think of the good things about New York as in some sense ours. We have proprietary feelings about the Metropolitan Opera, the Rockettes, the Statue of Liberty and, yes, the World Trade Center. We feel attached to them whether we've seen them or not (and we may actually be more likely than the natives to have visited them). To say that those who destroyed the Twin Towers attacked New York City is like calling an assault on Mount Rushmore an attack on South Dakota.

But there's something more going on here. The aftermath of September 11 reminded us that the New Yorkers we most often hear from are not the only people who live there. When southerners and other outsiders dislike (or fawn on) "New Yorkers," the people they usually have in mind are the media and show-business figures, politicians, business titans, and intellectuals they encounter on television—in short, "the people who run things." Sophisticated, worldly, cosmopolitan, if you admire them; supercilious, smug, arrogant, if you don't.

These people are still there, of course, and they sure can grate. Shortly after September 11, I heard Fran Leibowitz making snide comments on NPR about President Bush's reference to the "folks" responsible for the attacks. She apparently had that word associated with hayrides. But many of these obnoxious figures have been uncharacteristically subdued since last fall, and the attacks have highlighted a different kind of New Yorker, one many southerners and other Americans find more sympathetic.

To say that those who destroyed the Twin Towers attacked New York City is like calling an assault on Mount Rushmore an attack on South Dakota. Photograph courtesy of the National Park Service.

The bond between southerners and northern "good old boys" often has to do with sports. Head coach Frank McGuire, from Queens, steered the North Carolina Tar Heels basketball team to an undefeated season and a national championship, before taking the coaching job at the University of South Carolina. Here McGuire's 1956 team celebrates victory in the Dixie Classic. Photograph courtesy of the North Carolina Collection, Wilson Library, the University of North Carolina at Chapel Hill.

There has always been more to New York City than the "people who run things." Ever since the heyday of Jacksonian Democracy, an on-again off-again alliance has existed between ordinary southerners (that is, most of us) and New York's working people (that is, most of them). After the Civil War and Reconstruction, this coalition was famously described as one of "rum, Romanism and rebellion." Later, it elected Franklin Roosevelt to four terms. Later still, it re-assembled to elect Richard Nixon and Ronald Reagan.

Most southerners who know New York (I lived there for five years) know that there's a kind of outer-borough New York guy we get along with just fine. He is working-class and usually Irish, Jewish, or Italian, but these days sometimes black or Latino. He is what historian Paul Fussell called a "high prole," largely defined by his skills and "pride and a conviction of independence." When Mr. Fussell

Their accents may sound funny to southern ears, but they're our kind of Yankee: unpretentious, hard working when they have to be, offhandedly courageous. Heroes. Photograph by Tom Sperduto, courtesy of the U.S. Coast Guard.

identifies disdain for social climbing, fondness for hunting and gambling and sports, and unromantic attitudes toward women as his other traits, southerners should recognize the northern variety of what we used to call a "good old boy" (before the label escaped captivity and lost all precision). "A solid, reliable, unpretentious, stand-up, companionable, appropriately loose, joke-sharing feller," in the description of Roy Blount Jr.

The bond between southerners and this kind of northerner often does have to do with sports. Recall that "Broadway Joe" Namath of the New York Jets, the Pennsylvanian who became an archetypal New Yorker, launched his public persona as "Joe Willie" Namath of the Alabama Crimson Tide. (Mr. Namath even played a Confederate soldier in a seriously bad movie called *The Last Rebel*.)

Or consider Coach Frank McGuire, from St. Xavier High School and St. John's University in Queens, who steered the North Carolina Tar Heels basketball team to an undefeated season and a national championship, and later coached at South Carolina. The New York players McGuire recruited used to bemuse the locals with their habit of crossing themselves before foul shots. And then there's

Coach Jimmy Valvano of North Carolina State University, another New Yorker who led a southern team to a national championship and endeared himself even to fans of rival teams with his good-old-boy humor. (After his team blew a lead to lose to the archrival Tar Heels, Valvano claimed a fan wrote him "If you ever do that again, I'll come over and shoot your dog." Valvano said he wrote back saying he didn't have a dog, and the man replied: "I'm sending you a dog. But don't get too attached to him.")

These are the kinds of New Yorkers we saw on television after September 11: policemen, firemen, rescue workers—ordinary folks. Their accents may have sounded funny to southern ears, but they're our kind of Yankee: unpretentious, hard working when they have to be, offhandedly courageous.

Rudy Giuliani may or may not be one of them by nature, but in that context he sure looked it, and most of us found him wholly admirable. The post-9/11 fortitude and determination of New York's plain folk has led many of us to conclude that Tom Wolfe was wrong when, in one of his most famous essays, he described the stockcar racer Junior Johnson, from Ingle Hollow, Wilkes County, North Carolina, as "the last American hero." We have learned that there are some guys from places like Red Hook, Brooklyn, New York, who qualify as well.

NOTE

Reprinted with permission from *The American Enterprise*, a magazine of politics, business, and culture, www.taemag.com.

Yankee Interloper and Native Son:
Carl Carmer and Clarence Cason
Unlikely Twins of Alabama Exposé

by Philip Beidler

*I*n the early 1930s, Carl Carmer and Clarence Cason wrote two remarkably similar, controversial cultural exposés of early-twentieth-century Alabama—*Stars Fell on Alabama* (1934) and *90 Degrees in the Shade* (1935). One author was a cultural outsider; the other was an Alabamian born and bred. Yet despite this difference, the shared cultural fable they fashioned became an intensely southern story: both humorous and dark, teasing and haunted, absurd and poignant to the point of being lurid in Carmer's case and even tragic in Cason's. Moreover, the authors' strangely intertwined destinies, down to the similarities of their names and the comparable subjects and timing of their books, are marked by biographical and literary coincidences hardly seen in fiction, not to mention history. Yet their story is equally important as a parable of numerous intensely human missed connections and ill-imagined mirrorings as well—the ironies of a peculiarly southern *and* peculiarly modern set of meanings and morals.

The setting was Tuscaloosa, Alabama, once a bustling river town and site of the state's old frontier capital, but by the 1930s a sleepy, middle-sized city distinguished mainly by the dual presences of the state university and the state hospital for the insane. The principals were two writers of somewhat sensational and high-profile cultural critiques of life in early twentieth-century Alabama, books that received substantial attention not only within the state and the region but on the national scene as well. Both authors were born in the decade just before the turn of the century, both saw military duty in France during World War I, and both achieved considerable visibility as University of Alabama faculty members. The first was a young New Yorker named Carl Carmer, who arrived at the university in 1921 and spent the next six years teaching in the English department. The second was a native Alabamian, Clarence Cason, a 1917 graduate of the university and a member of the journalism faculty from 1928 until his untimely death in 1935.

Beyond these comparisons, however, visible similarities markedly diminish. Carmer was a true scion of the great Northeast, a graduate of Hamilton College

The authors of two highly controversial books on twentieth-century Alabama, Carl Carmer and Clarence Cason missed each other as faculty members at the University of Alabama at Tuscaloosa by just one year. Their lives and the books they wrote could not have had more in common — or have been more different. The University of Alabama campus in the 1930s, courtesy of the Oscar D. Cully Jr. Collection, W. S. Hoole Special Collections Library, the University of Alabama.

with a master's in English from Harvard. Styled by his students as a "'missionary of Eastern culture'" as well as "'one of those damn-Yankee professors who lectures on poetry and goes without a hat,'" he came to be regarded as a charming interloper, or in many quarters something a good deal worse. If a Yankee, at least he came with the kind of colonial pedigree southerners could respect—an upstate New Yorker descended from the old Dutch patroons. Handsome, likeable, nicely turned-out, he was a well-bred sophisticate who ran with a fast crowd and was himself something of an operator. With a somewhat older wife, said to be of wealthy background, he made his home in a neighborhood called the Highlands, the town's fashionable and expensive new suburb. He played golf and tennis at the country club and enjoyed dances and drinking parties, frequently unattended by his wife. In fact, as a literary barometer of domestic attachment, amidst the various journeys and adventures recorded by the somewhat raffish first-person narrator in his book, the spouse likewise went unmentioned. Perhaps this was as it should be, since by 1934 a new wife's name appeared on the dedication page of *Stars Fell on Alabama*.[1]

The Yankee interloper and the native son. While Carl Carmer, "one of those damn-Yankee professors who lectures on poetry and goes without a hat," left the University of Alabama at Tuscaloosa amidst rumors of impropriety, native Alabaman Clarence Cason was, by all accounts, a well-liked family man. Photograph of Cason (left), courtesy of Jane Cason Simpson; sketch of Carmer (right) by Allene G. Hatch.

Carmer's classroom specialty, poetry writing, was one that surely made the manly young easterner seem romantic to students of a literary bent—both male and female—and his work frequently pitted him as a rival of the English department's other resident cosmopolitan and charismatic teacher, Hudson Strode. When Carmer left in 1927, it was under a cloud of scandal. Consensus remains that the matter involved a female student. One account has it that a traffic stop revealed the young woman in the back seat of the professor's car in a state of incriminating undress. Another suggests that the young woman was one in whom Strode felt a strongly proprietary interest. [2]

Clarence Cason, by contrast, was a native son, Alabamian to the core and a model citizen if God ever made one. Born in Ragland, he grew up the son of a country doctor in Talladega and took his undergraduate degree at the university in Tuscaloosa. After service in World War I and experience as a working journalist with papers in Birmingham, Louisville, Washington, and New York, he earned a master's in English literature at the University of Wisconsin in 1925 and taught for three years at the University of Minnesota before returning to his alma mater. He was a devoted husband and an adoring father, with the family home in the old part of town near the country club. As a founding member of the university's vigorous new journalism department, he was respected and affectionately regarded by his students and colleagues. He also enjoyed the good opinion and good fellowship of the journalism community around the state, who knew him by the curious nickname Chico. It was, indeed, by that affectionate name that his friend, the prominent Alabama editorialist James Saxon Childers, bade him farewell in the pages of the *Birmingham News Age-Herald*—along with a glowing review of *90 Degrees in the Shade*—when Cason took his own life just days before the official release of the book for public sale.[3]

Oddly enough, the lives of these two authors, so similarly occupied and writing books so alike in many respects, seem never for a moment to have intersected. It is almost as if fate contrived to make them just miss each other at every turn, with Cason's undergraduate years preceding Carmer's arrival, and Carmer's departure then occurring a year before Cason's return. As for the books themselves, their composition and reception followed similarly disconnected chronological and geographical patterns. Carmer was able to write his 1930s Alabama travelogue cum exposé from something of a distance, and although he contributed in print to public discussion attending its appearance—in a New York interview conducted by the visiting James Saxon Childers—he was nevertheless somewhat insulated by time and distance from the controversy. Cason, in contrast, wrote his book sitting at home, looking his subject and his likely audience full in the face. And, as Cason noted himself, he also wrote in awareness of Carmer's book and of the controversy attending its publication.

So then to the books themselves. As with the authors' biographies, it is at first the almost uncanny array of similarities that catches the eye. Both books announce themselves through titles and jacket copy that suggest a sense of breathless regional allure, and, as historian Wayne Flynt has observed, both were written accordingly in "a sprightly, popular style."[4] Even design features seem to mirror each other. Both jackets are a vivid yellow and green, and both feature wraparound, somewhat art deco depictions of intensely southern settings. The jacket for Carmer's *Stars Fell on Alabama* has us peering into a cane thicket through which a man drives a buckboard. Cason's jacket cover features towering, moss-draped oaks and a meandering river, a dozing angler on the bank blissfully inattentive to his bobber and line. The page layout of both books likewise demonstrates that much attention was devoted to artistic design. Carmer's text, from the New York trade publisher Farrar and Rinehart, was a lavish production heavily dependent throughout on visual atmospherics, with author Carmer and illustrator LeRoy Baldridge in fact given equal billing. One is struck even today, for instance, by the hauntingly beautiful depiction in the book's endpapers of the legendary 1830s meteor shower referred to in the title. The frontispiece is a hand-drawn map of the state, an exotic preview of the regions to be depicted: "The Red Hills" and "Foothills" to the North, "The Black Belt" and "Conjure" and "Cajan" countries to the South. The facing title page features an imposing Greek

*The surface similarities between Cason's and Carmer's lives are reflected in the original dust jackets of their books. Both covers share color schemes and both picture scenes of a recognizably southern rural environment. Courtesy of the University of North Carolina Press (*90 Degrees in the Shade*) and The Rare Book Collection, the University of North Carolina at Chapel Hill (*Stars Fell on Alabama*).*

revival mansion in long romantic perspective. Likewise, each of the book's main sections announces itself with a highly evocative illustration. "Tuscaloosa Nights" shows a Klan cross-burning; "In the Red Hills," a scene from a backwoods fiddlers' convention; "Black Belt," a sultry beauty posed against the backdrop of a plantation house; "Conjure Country," an aged black woman toiling at her cauldron; "Mobile and the Bayou Country," a vista of tropical palm trees and waves along the gulf; "Cajan," another young woman, this time posed on the porch of a weathered shack; and "From the Author's Note Book," a solitary rustic on a mule, a rifle across the saddle, his hound trailing.

Cason's *90 Degrees in the Shade* was from the University of North Carolina Press, primarily a publisher of academic books. Still, it did not stint on illustration. Here the emphasis is photographic, with Edward Rice the artist. Two to four plates appear in each section and, when possible, illustrate topics under discussion. For instance, photographs of scenes from the lives of the rural poor, black and white, appear in a chapter titled "Shadows of the Plantation." Most of the illustrations found in "Black Figures in the Sun" depict the toil and poverty of African American sharecroppers and wage laborers. In other cases, the images are generally atmospheric. Tuscaloosans, for example, would have recognized a number of ar-

Cason called one of the chapters of 90 Degrees in the Shade *"Shadows of the Plantation." A plantation house in afternoon gloom, courtesy of the North Carolina Collection, Wilson Library, the University of North Carolina at Chapel Hill.*

chitectural landmarks, including the Gorgas House on the university campus and the Jemison, Cochrane, and Drish houses in the old downtown. The caption for the Cochrane house photograph notes that the building served "as the library of Stillman Institute, a school for negroes in Tuscaloosa, Alabama." The Drish house, described as "a beautiful old Southern mansion of Italian Renaissance architecture," is pictured serving its forlorn new duty as an auto parts business.

In both cases, chapter headings and subtitles tend to lean heavily on exotic verbal hyperventilation. Within individual sections, Carmer, for instance, indulged in such lurid subtitles as "Flaming Cross," "God in the Canebrake," "Conjure Woman," and "Lynching." The last, it should be added, lives up fully to its title, being an account of an outbreak of horrific racial violence while Carmer is the guest of his Black Belt friends, "Knox" and "Mary Louise"—a pogrom-like orgy of random murder that claimed among its sweep of black victims an elderly woman and a venerable, much-beloved preacher. More happily located on the regional charm scale, Carmer's historical account of the Vine and Olive colony at Demopolis becomes "Plaisant Pais de France." Legends of Railroad Bill, Rube Burrow, and others appear under the title "The Tombigbee Outlaws." Nor did the generally less flashy Cason stint, at least on chapter heads. "It Never Snows" was followed by "Shadows of the Plantation," "Garlands of Straw," "Fascism, Southern Style," "Black Figures in the Sun," and others of similar tone. A penultimate chapter on the ownership class of a rising industrial South is titled "They are Not All Monsters." A final meditation on the peculiar intractability of many of the region's most severe problems is called "The Philosopher's Stone."

As suggested by such topical parallels, the two books are remarkably consonant in their identification of the particular cultural ills endemic to the region. Social problems include agricultural poverty, industrial underdevelopment, economic inequality, political demagoguery, religious intransigence, educational backwardness, racial bigotry. Both books address southern chauvinism, xenophobia, defensiveness, and reliance on traditional wisdom; a habitual quickness to perceive insult; a chronic retreat into hostile closed-mindedness; and a congenital tendency to use violence as a first resort in attending to matters of personal disagreement and political controversy.

Again, however, as with the authors, so with the texts: if it is the surface similarities that first catch the eye, it is equally the differences that arrest and fascinate. And chief among these differences is each author's distinctive narrative voice. Carmer's *Stars Fell on Alabama* is first and foremost the work of an observer and recorder. Carmer is always a stranger in a strange land, fascinated, bemused, and—like many a Yankee sojourner in the region—more than occasionally horrified. Carmer is markedly inside the text as he experiences the various regions he visits and their inhabitants; but he is also decidedly outside, not so much reflecting on what he sees as colorfully registering it, the poet as traveling ethnologist, scribbling on his pad, reporting from the field. To be sure, he reports on social problems. The coexistence of poverty alongside tremendous wealth, of ignorance alongside a graceful traditional culture, the violence that seems to lie just under the surface of everyday life—bootlegging, lynching, fundamentalism, superstition, ignorance. Upon his arrival at the university, one of the first admonitions Carmer received from a fellow faculty member was to get out before it was too late. Yet, as Wayne Flynt has noted, Alabama cast for Carmer its peculiar spell of enchantment, a world not so much of social and political practices as of elemental folkways. (Indeed, it is said that he first intended the extensive notes he took during the period to be the basis for a scholarly article in an anthropological journal.) Accordingly, the organization is loose, paralleling his visits to the various regions of the state, with length of entry frequently dictated by the degree of per-

opposite:

While both books exposed the underbelly of Alabama's social and cultural life, Cason's 90 Degrees in the Shade *contained an especially bleak portrayal of the Depression-era poor in Alabama—both African American and white. 1930s Alabama, photographed by Arthur Rothstein (above) and Marion Post Walcott (below), both from the collections of the Library of Congress.*

sonal fascination or social bonhomie. As might be expected—again, not the first time it happened to a Yankee—Carmer was mesmerized by the Black Belt. Of the six major sections of the book, the one so titled is twice as long as its nearest competitors and four times as long as several others.

If the organization is loose, the method is decidedly literary—even to some extent, as journalist Howell Raines has noted, rather liberally fictionalized. Carmer's frequent guide, the intellectual, worldly, northern educated yet deeply southern and deeply cynical "Knox," for instance, is actually a composite character, partly Judge Bernard Harwood of Tuscaloosa and partly a university student, Knox Ide, from Anniston. "Mary Louise," a beautiful, artistically gifted Black Belt matron, is similarly modeled with some fictional license on the remarkable Alabama folklorist, Ruby Pickens Tartt. Her fictionalized husband, "Tennant," an acerbic young attorney and landowner, seems to have derived largely from a Mobile acquaintance named Tennant Griffin. Accordingly, the book's story line often reads in many ways like a novel, a fascinating combination of anecdotal compilation and racy travelogue. Carmer's vivid retelling of well-known tales combines with his own adventures: at a Klan rally in Tuscaloosa, at a fiddlers' convention and sacred harp singing in the Red Hills, at a Greene County political barbecue—with any given occasion likely to be flavored with liberal amounts of white whiskey provided by his traveling companions. Across the state—in city, town, and hamlet—Carmer employs the artist's skill for social panorama. Brisk, bumptious, nouveau-everything Birmingham rises from its mountains of coal and iron; Mobile presides like an exotic grand dowager along the gulf. In between Carmer gives us his landscapes, his legends, his tours of great houses; he novelistically reproduces the dialogues, the accents, the spicy interplay of voices, white and black, rich and poor, genteel and roughhewn, profane and sacred, cosmopolitan and provincial. And so he admitted of himself and his book in an epilogue. "Like a character in imaginative fiction, I feel that I stepped into a past that lives and is concurrent with today."[5]

In contrast, Cason's perspective in *90 Degrees in the Shade* is that of impassioned discursive engagement. To be sure, there is some personal testimony and anecdote, often supplying some of the book's most compelling and poignant moments. At a Tuscaloosa carnival with his daughter, for instance, Cason wonders at the easy mingling of races on a Ferris wheel, as opposed to the bitter segregation prevailing just outside on the street during an average business day. He likewise records with horror the particulars of no fewer than four vigilante-style racial murders within the county during the past year. But overall, the mode of Cason's book is essay and argument. Here is a man who was not only intimately part of the society he depicted, but who also applied a high level of critical analysis to that culture. The point of the book is the serious discussion of major socio-economic and political issues: poverty, racism, ignorance, demagoguery, mindless

hatred, lawless violence. Particular practices that come in for attention include the sharecropping system, with its unfair mortgage practices and loan-sharking; the exploitative labor policies and union-busting associated with the mill system; and the hideous double standard of justice perpetuated by lynch law. On some matters, Cason may have ridden a particular thesis farther than it could take him. On the issue of climate, for instance, Cason describes the white southerner's appreciation of heat as incentive for an afternoon's fishing or game of golf. Like everyone else, Cason surely failed to see the future of the Sunbelt, with air-conditioning as the engine of its economic miracle. But he was dead right on race, with "shadows of the plantation" continuing to be the operative metaphor, and in Alabama, at least, he was also sadly correct on the persistence of demagoguery, which he aptly defined as the political art "of promising the people everything and getting them nothing."[6] Likewise, he clearly diagnosed the efforts of political and economic elites, continuing to this day, to dominate the laboring poor, black and white, on the principle of divide and conquer.

At the same time, if Carmer could be literary without being frivolous, Cason could be serious without seeming needlessly dour and professorial. In fact, he had a lively sense of humor, and he wasn't scared to use it, with some of his most telling observations remaining his most humorously quotable. On the literary predilections of his regional compatriots, he noted, for example, "The southerner reads the morning newspaper because he wants to know about the Society events and the election campaigns, which he regards in somewhat the same light; but he thinks books are suitable for invalids." And on the daily rough and tumble of politics, he allowed, "For some years I have been harboring the ridiculous notion that articles on election campaigns in the South, as well as all partisan editorials on the subject, should be printed on the sports pages of the newspapers." On the secular influence of the southern clergy, he spoke with gimlet-eyed precision: "The slipper of the Anglican divine moves in earnest grace across the ballroom floor at country clubs, and the heavier foot of the Calvinist regularly marks the turf on many a putting green. Any slackening of churchward procession in recent years has been compensated by a concourse of ministers around the festive noontide board of Kiwanis. Mohammed has gone to the mountain."[7]

One final difference remains to be noted between these mid-1930s books, perhaps the crucial one. And that is that Carmer's is actually in many ways a very 1920s book, with much of the jazz age about it. This probably should not surprise us, given the time of the authorial sojourn in Alabama that gave rise to it. Still, in their mingling with Alabamians of various descriptions across the state, Carmer and his own social set bear a pronounced resemblance to F. Scott Fitzgerald flappers and philosophers. Not for nothing, after all, was Zelda herself from Montgomery. There is a desperate gaiety there, the search for the next party, the solace of a golden disillusionment laid out against the larger prospect of a declining order, with nothing but a sterile modernist hubbub and bustle to put in its place. Likewise, it remains a text almost automatically associated with the popular Mitchell Parrish and Frank Perkins song inspired by the title. Substitute white lightning for bathtub gin, cotillion clubs for speakeasies, and the equation is nearly complete. In contrast, the Depression broods over Cason's book, supplying a somber, documentary mood. This is the South of the Scottsboro Trial, the Tennessee Valley Authority, the sharecropping poor soon to reappear in *Let Us Now Praise Famous Men*. Likewise, the photographs frequently have a Walker Evans quality that would not have made them seem out of place in the latter text. Even the chapter titles suggest a period grimness: "Garlands of Straw," "Fascism, Southern Style," "The Machine's Last Frontier."

Finally, of course, we come to the critical receptions. In both cases, the books proved controversial; at the same time, in both cases, response was not nearly as negative as might have been imagined—or as has been, for that matter, popularly recorded. Northern commentators, of course, generally praised Carmer, although ironically suggesting a certain sentimental bias in the book toward his adopted home and its friendly people. The opinions of southern reviewers, on the other hand, were predictably mixed, and on controversial particulars frequently defensive, if not vociferously hostile. Alabama responses, often at the visceral level of letters to the editor and guest opinion pieces, expressed outrage at Carmer's abuse of trust, hospitality, friendship. It seemed just what an interloping damn Yankee professor would do, the common opinion seemed to run, especially one whose leave-taking was clouded by salacious rumor and scandal. Surprising, on the other hand—then and now—was official literary opinion, which proved mainly affirmative, with progressive editorialists such as James Saxon Childers and John Temple Graves of Birmingham and Grover Hall of Montgomery testifying to the book's worthiness as a salutary kind of cultural wake-up call. Indeed, if anything—a matter surely not lost on Clarence Cason—the curiously distinguishing feature of journalism wars springing up around Carmer's book seemed to be the sheer amount of vitriol visited on any card-carrying southerner who had the temerity to claim in print not only that much of what Carmer said was true, but also that it should require all Alabamians of intelligence and good will to take a correspondingly good look at themselves and the state. Like Carmer, it was

Whereas Yankee Carl Carmer could be dismissed as a latter-day carpetbagger, Clarence Cason was a native Alabamian who fit in well at Tuscaloosa. After graduating from the University of Alabama in 1917, he returned to his alma mater to teach from 1928 until his death in 1935. Photograph of a young Cason, courtesy of Jane Cason Simpson.

suggested, perhaps they too should be subjected to inquiries about their motives at the very least, if not in fact their parentage. A simple equation of loyalties seemed to be implied, and again it was surely one that Cason must have noted and taken deeply to heart: for a white Alabama writer in any way to defend Carmer or a book such as he had written was purely and simply to turn against one's own people.

Cason's reviews likewise reflected a certain mixture of response predicated largely upon schools of regional ideology. Northerners and writers generally in established intellectual journals again were extremely sympathetic and admiring. And southerners of the regionalist school, headquartered at the University of North Carolina, with which Cason had been affiliated, were also quite positive. One serious intellectual dissent by a southerner, on the other hand, came in a long, two-part article in the *New Republic*, where Mississippian Stark Young served as the designated mouthpiece of the Vanderbilt Agrarians. Within the state, there was hardly the outcry that Carmer's book had met. Reviews were somber and respectful, appreciative of the deeply personal reflections of a native southerner on his people and his place. As with the measured response of Alabama progressives to Carmer, here an even more affirmative keynote was struck by Childers, who called *90 Degrees in the Shade* "a book filled with quiet wisdom and a gentle love for the South and for Southern men and women."[8]

The chief difference, of course, as noted in a shocked addendum to Childers's glowing prepublication review, was that Clarence Cason wasn't around to see it. On May 8, 1935, just three days before the public release of *90 Degrees in the Shade*, he killed himself, and surely some, if not much, of his mental disquietude came from his firsthand witness to the controversy, such as it was, over Carmer's book as he worked to complete his own. On the other hand, mere journalistic controversy couldn't have done it for a man of Clarence Cason's character, experience, and proven mettle. For one thing, despite his university faculty status, he was hardly your average academic hothouse flower, but rather a seasoned veteran of the journalism scene and as well regarded by his Alabama newspaper cohorts as by his fellow faculty members and students. In addition, he was a practiced southern controversialist, having tried out virtually all of the major ideas and topics of social critique in prominent venues north and south, including the *New Republic*, the *North American Review*, the *New York Times Magazine*, *Yale Review*, *Virginia Quarterly Review*, and *South Atlantic Quarterly*. His own loyalties were well known, siding with the progressive University of North Carolina regionalists against what he regarded as the retrograde Vanderbilt Agrarian nostalgist-elitists, which was the message he sent by choosing North Carolina's press as his publisher. Cason, too, had not been at all timid about taking his stand.

One certainly cannot discount completely the idea Cason may have entertained of actual physical danger to himself or to his family. In the mid 1930s, the

Tuscaloosa Klan was still in full cry, likely perpetrators of the recent lynchings in the city and county about which Cason had written in graphic detail and for which no indictments had ever been returned. Also, as journalist and critic Bailey Thompson records, just the year before a professor at Alabama College in Montevallo visiting in Tuscaloosa had in fact been accosted by forty hooded Klansmen and subjected to a search of his car.[9] To be sure, the perpetrators of such acts were not likely readers of his book or even of reviews or editorial comment. Moreover, on race, even as a progressive thinker, Cason's view was that of a fairly conventional southerner of the era. On the other hand, one need only recall the Wallace-era tribulations, both spiritual and physical, of native son and Republican judge Frank Johnson—famously derided by his former friend the governor as an "integratin', carpetbaggin', scalawaggin' bald-faced liar"—to wonder just how little inducement it might have taken for the white-sheeted local illuminati to set themselves to work on a hometown university professor rumored to be guilty of similar infractions.

Finally, as a southern intellectual and working journalist, Cason surely must have been transfixed by a particular feature of the Carmer controversy: how quickly hostile critical opinion coalesced around Carmer's status as a treacherous outsider. After all, the general sentiment seemed to run, what was one to expect? Who was he but a glad-handing Yankee ingrate who had ill-repaid the hospitality of Alabamians rich and poor, great and small, who had once opened their doors and their hearts to him? Certainly he was no gentleman—and according to ru-

A short time later in his classic The Mind of the South, *W. J. Cash, himself an eventual suicide, wrote: "Poor Clarence Cason . . . who felt compelled to commit suicide, in part at least because of the fear of the fiercely hostile attitude which he knew that both the school authorities and his fellow faculty members would take toward his criticisms of the South in his* 90 Degrees in the Shade." *W. J. Cash, courtesy of the Photography Collection of the Harry Ransom Humanities Research Center, the University of Texas at Austin.*

mors of his abrupt dismissal from the university faculty, perhaps something of a rapscallion or worse. Now Cason could not be subject to any of these accusations. On the other hand, he surely must have known how likely he was to be accused of another kind of betrayal, and that of course was precisely the kind of personal and cultural treachery that had already been ascribed to many of Carmer's local defenders—not only betrayal from within, but also betrayal of the southern cultural insider's peculiar code of noblesse oblige and forbearance in criticizing the shortcomings of one's own people and place. In essence, Cason likely felt himself about to be accused of betrayal as a violation of southern honor. For in writing a book like Carmer's that subjected Alabama and Alabamians, frequently by name and place, to intense and often unfavorable critical scrutiny and then publishing it for all the world to see, a native Alabamian like Cason might be said to have committed nothing less than treason against his own kind.

Nor, as evidenced by common journalistic practice, was this a kind of cultural reflex that had to be imagined, least of all by a Clarence Cason. At the height of the Carmer controversy, for instance, the July 7, 1934, *Montgomery Advertiser* also found time for another Yankee critic of the state, John Howard Lawson, whose "unsalted propaganda drama" about the Scottsboro trials, *They Shall Not Die,* earned him branding as a "a professional jackass who makes it pay." Even worse contempt, however, was reserved that same month for expatriate southerner and Pulitzer Prize-winning novelist T. S. Stribling, now nestled, as the paper noted, among "the Yankees, who love to be fooled." "Stribling Shuns Alabama," read the July 2 caption. And underneath the photo, the article explained why he probably needed to. "Perhaps Stribling would not be so embarrassed today if his first book of North Alabama folk had been accepted at its true value—as fiction from a mind that is in love with sewage fantasy." Most germane to our purposes was an item of August 3, 1934, the report of a talk given by Clarence Cason himself to the Birmingham Rotary Club. Its title: "The Sensitive South." Its subject: the irrational defensiveness of contemporary southerners to any and all negative depictions of life in the region.

Whatever Cason's thoughts on the general climate of his book's reception, in the end, as Bailey Thomson has definitively shown, it was the particular likelihood of comparisons between *Stars Fell on Alabama* and *90 Degrees in the Shade* that not only preoccupied Cason but seemed increasingly a source of genuine horror. The book's jacket, for instance, prompted a hasty telegram to W. T. Couch, director of the University of North Carolina Press, warning that a reference to Carmer's book would reinflame old Tuscaloosa resentments concerning Carmer and his depiction of the university as lacking in intellectual life. Couch wired back, trying to offer comfort, but it was too late.[10]

For by now, as with the fictional suicide of South-haunted Quentin Compson in William Faulkner's *The Sound and the Fury*, published only a few years before, perhaps death for Cason just simply had come to look like the only way out, the only way to stop saying over and over, as he imagined he would certainly have to, "I don't hate it! I don't hate it! I don't! I don't." As noted by critic Fred Hobson, this was certainly the implication of the death of Cason's fellow regionalist, W. J. Cash, himself an eventual suicide under comparably mysterious circumstances, writing a short time later in *his* classic work of cultural analysis, *The Mind of the South*. "Poor Clarence Cason," Cash had observed in his manuscript, "who taught journalism at Alabama" and who "felt compelled to commit suicide, in part at least because of his fear of the fiercely hostile attitude which he knew that both the school authorities and his fellow faculty members would take toward his criticisms of the South in his *90 Degrees in the Shade*."[11]

The nagging question remains: just what would have happened had the appearance of Cason's book not been presaged by the controversy over Carmer's? The only problem with an answer is, of course, that Cason's tragic death renders it intellectually moot, if not morally irrelevant. To put this more bluntly, it was Clarence Cason, late on the afternoon of May 8, 1935, who elected to end his life with a self-inflicted gunshot, and it is we, several generations after, who can now merely begin to speculate about meanings, motives, morals — and even then, only with due respect for a wise and good fellow human whose very wisdom and goodness, in this case, seem ironically to have propelled him to his final agony.

Whatever happened, we know this. Carl Carmer, Mr. Outside, could write

"The South has a way of tormenting those who care most about her," and perhaps Clarence Cason saw suicide as the only way out of the anguish of having criticized the land he ardently loved — the only way to avoid having forever to shout with Faulkner's Quentin Compson, "I don't hate it! I don't hate it! I don't! I don't." Photograph of Clarence Cason, courtesy of Jane Cason Simpson.

about the South in the spirit of Kiss and Tell. In contrast, Clarence Cason couldn't have stopped being Mr. Inside if he wanted to. Clarence Cason's love for the South was the kind of love that cannot exist without deep spiritual commitment. For only such love, as one reviewer rightly noted, can produce such writers: "neither angry Puritans, writing of an impure and perfect South with all the detailed violence of a backwoods evangelist describing sin, nor as the earlier lazy literary cavaliers, who refused to see any vestige of loan sharks or pellagra in the jessamine-scented moonlight," but rather, writers with the bravery to "see beauty and hate evil on the same street in the same South where both do in truth exist." Now Carmer's book certainly tells us this as well. In his Alabama, too, the grotesque, violent, and lurid repel and attract us precisely because of how often they nestle amidst enchantment, grace, and beauty: "the hedonism existing side by side with the puritanism," as Bailey Thomson put it in a *Huntsville Times* editorial more than three decades later, "the ever-present violence dwelling just below the calm surface, the indifference to things intellectual, the great homage paid to female chastity and the equally great preoccupation with love-making, the casual sensuousness of black culture with the great formality of the white. This and much more Carmer described."[12] At this remove, one should probably refrain from moral preachment on literary positioning; it is enough to conclude simply that both books could finally be said to be in character. Both writers, that is, simply wrote and published the books they thought they had to write. For Carmer, a visitor, Alabama was material. Material is what writers write about. And to his credit, he would also go on over a long career to write with characteristic charm and engagement on a variety of subjects, including characters from American folklore and the early history of his own native New York. As a literary citizen, his record would be equally distinguished, including presidencies of the American Authors' Guild, the Poetry Society of America, the McDowell Writers' Colony, and the American Center of P.E.N., the International Society of Writers and Editors. For Clarence Cason, a native son, on the other hand, Alabama was home. As Alabamian Wayne Flynt, himself no small authority on a native son's lifelong lover's quarrel with the land of his birth, wrote of Cason in a recent essay, "Like a fickle lover, the South has a way of tormenting those who care most about her."[13]

NOTES

1. Carl Carmer, *Stars Fell on Alabama* (Farrar and Rinehart, 1934), introduction by J. Wayne Flynt (reprint, University of Alabama Press, 1985), 11. Howell Raines, "This Strange Country," *Virginia Quarterly Review* 66 (1990): 296–97.

2. *Ibid.*, 304.

3. James Saxon Childers, "The Book is Closed," *Birmingham News Age-Herald*, 19 May 1935, 8.

4. Flynt, "Introduction," *Stars*, xvii.

5. Raines, "Strange Country," 297–98, 303–304; Carmer, *Stars*, 270.

6. Clarence Cason, *90 Degrees in the Shade* (University of North Carolina Press, 1935), introduction by J. Wayne Flynt (reprint, University of Alabama Press, 1983), 89.

7. Cason, *90 Degrees*, 10, 72, 65.

8. James Saxon Childers, "A Splendid Book About the South," *Birmingham News Age-Herald*, 19 May 1935, 8.

9. Bailey Thomson, "Clarence Cason: Journalist in Academe," *Alabama Review* 35 (July 2000): 195. For a detailed account of the grisly 1933 lynchings and the Klan harassment a year later of the Montevallo professor, J. R. Steelman, see Glenn Feldman, *Politics, Society, and the Klan in Alabama, 1915–49* (University of Alabama Press, 1999), 251–54.

10. Thomson, "Clarence Cason," 194.

11. Fred Hobson, *Tell About the South: The Southern Rage to Explain* (Louisiana State University Press, 1978), 356; W. J. Cash, *The Mind of the South* (1941; reprint Vintage, 1960), 334.

12. Jonathan Daniels, "Southern Testament," *Saturday Review of Literature*, 6 July 1935, 14; Bailey Thomson, "Stars Fell on Alabama and a Young Easterner," *Huntsville Times*, 26 September 1976, 15.

13. Flynt, "Introduction," *90 Degrees*, v.

In Search of the Lost Confederate Graveyard

The Last Civil War Correspondent Enters the Field

photographs by Charlie Curtis

It would be a two-mile trek through the seldom traveled woods outside Front Royal, Virginia, and it could easily result in a futile search for something no more than myth. As a known regional photographer, Curtis had been tipped by locals to a setting that, he said, "brought to mind the truly amazing." Hopeful, eager—and wary, too, of the disappointment he would experience if he could not find the fabled place—Curtis set out into the cold and gray countryside one day last winter in search of a lost cemetery for Confederate soldiers.

His journey began with the typical false starts you might expect from a trail marked by memories and hearsay, but then the woods suddenly seemed to calibrate itself to his journey. He found what he estimated to be a 140-year-old tree. If he was right about its age, it had been a sapling during the Civil War. He stopped to photograph its crown and then ventured on, believing he had discovered, in the ways of these Virginia woods, the first marker on the trail to lost Confederates.

After hiking three-quarters of a mile, Curtis turned off of an old dirt road already partly grown over by wild grasses. He was leaving the last landscape he would find that day that had not been completely allowed to reclaim itself from the people who once lived there. "Furious" was how he would later describe this land, as if the walk had become something akin to traveling the inner reaches of the mind. "It is beautiful," he thought, as he left the dirt road, "and menacing. No place you'd ever want to lay down to sleep."

Now past the pines, after having hiked another half mile, the man on the hunt for lost soldiers could not help but think of himself as hunted, too. Curtis knew he was trekking through hunters' territory, but finding these stands in the trees, even empty, still gave him a start. At first, he thought only of the absent hunter and his gun; then he quickly realized the similarity between the quest of the solitary huntsman, traveling through otherwise uninhabited terrain, and his own mission.

After several more minutes trudging through the forest, at last Curtis could sense that he was closing in on the lost Confederates. This truly was a woods full of graves—and other vestiges of the past. A fallen cedar in decay still bore the shards of its attachment to the ground and life. Forty-year-old cattle remains lay bleaching in open air. The cattle bones reminded Curtis of the old backwoods practice of dragging a dead cow away and out of view to allow it to decompose unburied. He had done it himself many years ago while growing up on a farm and knew that it was a harrowing and exhausting undertaking—something that you could sort of get used to, but that never was easy. It seemed that each step through these woods had become a step back in time. So on he walked for another hundred years.

And then, there they were, under a canopy of branches in deep woods, resolute in the undergrowth—and just as Francis Finch Miles had promised in his famous "The Blue and the Gray":

> Under the sod and the dew,
> Waiting the Judgment Day:
> Under the one, the Blue,
> Under the other, the Gray.

"I was overcome by the presence of the grave-markers of these men," Curtis later remembered. "As a documentary photographer, you want to preserve information for the viewer. But these men were part of one of the greatest conflicts in history, and now, in this setting, they were so much at peace. I only wanted to capture the essence of that place. And to understand what had led me to this intersection of truth and myth."

With his journey now at an end, this collection of four weather-worn gravestones from the Bennett, Steed, and Martin families reminded Charlie Curtis that these men—whose very names even were being lost in various stages of erosion—did more than fill out the lines and the numbers for Civil War historians. "We've analyzed ploys and tactics," Curtis says, "and we think we know causes and reasons. We think we know it all. But these were just men. They were George W. Martin, a corporal in the Virginia Infantry. George Martin and these men *were* the Civil War."

Touched by his discovery of the lost graveyard, Curtis nevertheless set about ful-
filling the primary mission of the documentary photographer—to capture information. When he returned from his visit to the hidden cemetery, he brought back
the names of the dead: Corporal George W. Martin, Company D, 49th Virginia
Infantry, Confederate States of America; Joseph Bennett, Company E, 7th Virginia Calvary, Confederate States of America; William Bennett, Company A, 18th
Virginia Calvary, Confederate States of America; and, James W. Steed, Company
B, 17th Virginia Regiment, Confederate States of America.

Heritage, not Hate?
Collecting Black Memorabilia

by Lynn Casmier-Paz

Turn-of-the-twentieth-century advertisers used images of African American children to promote products ranging from soap and stove polish to shoes and ginger. These and similar representations of African Americans now command high prices in a growing market. Item #A0428, Emergence of Advertising in America, 2000, Rare Book, Manuscript, and Special Collections Library, Duke University.

arly in my research on slave narratives and the popular imagination I was leafing through moldy magazines when I became transfixed by a proliferation of advertisements that used images of black children. At the back of the journals' yellowing pages, I saw blackened, tar-colored characters that were used to sell stove polish, black shoes, black thread—any domestic good that could be sold by exploiting the children's exaggerated blackness. The connection between these characters and the goods they advertised was not readily apparent to me then, and I became determined to understand their purpose. I started to photocopy those images wherever I saw them in magazines from around the turn of the twentieth century. It was not until later that I learned that my desire to collect these images had inadvertently placed me in the company of an elite, but controversial, group of African Americans who trade in these images and other objects, which they have labeled "black memorabilia."

I had seen such images before. When I was a child in the sixties, our family pilgrimages from St. Louis to visit our grandmother in New Orleans had been punctuated by Mammy dolls, grotesque figurines, and racist postcards in every truck-stop gift-shop along Highway 55. I had seen them even more recently when I drove Interstate 95 from my home in Orlando to defend my dissertation in Pittsburgh. Stops in North and South Carolina, often in the same stores that sell Confederate flags, revealed that the images are currently less abundant, but no less surprisingly racist.

More recently, such images have made it into the national mainstream. In Spike Lee's satirical film *Bamboozled*, for example, blackface minstrelsy and Aunt Jemima cookie jars serve as complex symbols of African American wealth, as well as battlegrounds for class struggle and violence.[1] Before the film lurched into the controversial arena of public opinion, I had no idea that these images I had seen in my youthful travels through the Deep South had achieved an entirely different audience. I had to head north to Silver Spring, Maryland, in order to find out their current value.

In April of 1998 I decided to learn more about the images by attending the Tenth Annual Black Memorabilia Showcase in Silver Spring. Since the images were so obviously derogatory, I prepared myself for what I believed would be a convention of collectors who were overwhelmed with nostalgia for lost white supremacy. Because I knew nothing about the images as "black memorabilia," I did not know who collected them, nor could I imagine why. As for myself, I was not a "collector." Rather, I was a *historian*, I reasoned, who had no intention of selling the grotesque images. I merely sought a historical understanding of my photocopies.

I was therefore stunned to learn that the Showcase was promoted and organized by Malinda Saunders—herself an African American. Moreover, when I ar-

"I SAY SNOW FLAKE, DAT STOVE WAS BLACKED WITH RISING SUN. DID YOU EBER SEE DE LIKE?"

Author Lynn Casmier-Paz was shocked to discover that the trade in racist memorabilia, involving surprisingly large amounts of money, was operated by African Americans. Item #A0452, Emergence of Advertising in America, 2000, Rare Book, Manuscript, and Special Collections Library, Duke University.

rived at the Silver Spring armory, I found the place jammed with brown and black people hawking rusted "Authentic Slave Shackles" that only a consumer with a platinum credit card could purchase. I paid a rotund brown woman the three-dollar entrance fee and walked in utter amazement past brown and black buyers and sellers of all ages, shapes, and sizes. Antique documents of manumission, Aunt Jemima pancake boxes ("mint-condition, headwrap image"), Jackson Five album covers, Michael Jordan posters, and grotesquely exaggerated racist ads were sold, bartered, and valued in the armory's multiple levels. My own ignorance about the current value and trade in these artifacts had come to the right place.

At the Silver Spring armory I learned that my photocopies are indeed considered to be "black memorabilia," and the originals are often worth hundreds, even thousands, of dollars. Currently, the trade in black memorabilia, which includes "black ephemera," or advertisements, has become a lucrative exchange whose goods have risen in value enormously in the past thirty years.

Even more interesting is the fact that black memorabilia has become big business due, in large part, to the contributions of African Americans. At the Showcase, and afterwards, I learned that even the most influential and prominent African Americans collect them. Collectors of black memorabilia include actor Bill Cosby, talk show host Oprah Winfrey, renowned historian Henry Louis Gates Jr., and civil rights activist Julian Bond, who has written a "Special Introduction" to the *Black Americana Price Guide*, a book I purchased at the Showcase.[2]

In his introduction, Bond explains the importance of black memorabilia for African Americans by saying it consists of nostalgic items that "remind today's collector of what was." He further states that his ownership of the items changes their meaning: "For others . . . these artifacts summon up yesterday's world, but in *our* hands and homes they become reminders of a different sort. They speak of triumph and overcoming, and inform *us* that despite what others thought and believed, *we* were never what they suggest" (emphasis mine).[3] Bond and other collectors believe that when African Americans collect artifacts that evidence grotesque representations of blackness—when the images are in "our" hands—their significance is transformed.

In *Bamboozled*, the character Sloan Hopkins (played by Jada Pinkett Smith) tells television producer Pierre Delecroix (played by Damon Dayans) that the grotesque items of black memorabilia serve as important "reminders" of "what they thought of us." When she celebrates his success with the gift of an authentic, turn-of-the-century "Nigger Bank," she helps him to understand the objectives of bourgeois African American collectors. "It's not a repro," Sloan explains. That the item is not a reproduction means that the value of the authentic bank is, according to price guides, one thousand dollars. In a single gesture, Sloan offers a gift of both history and wealth—a "reminder" that, not coincidentally, both increases Delecroix's net worth and symbolizes his success.

The "reminder," "triumph," and "overcoming" that black memorabilia collecting represents to African Americans is markedly different from black memorabilia's meaning for Dawn Reno. Reno is a white Florida collector and writer whose *Encyclopedia of Black Collectibles* states that "collecting black memorabilia will arouse *your* emotions" (my emphasis). She ends her introduction to the revised edition with a cheerful suggestion that one should "enjoy" collecting racist artifacts. However, Reno's cheer is followed by grave advice when she tells the collector to "remember that education is of utmost importance, for it is the one thing that will finally erase the lines of discrimination and prejudice."[4]

What is significant about Reno's disposition toward collecting black memorabilia is the absence of a personal, intimate connection to the artifacts. Since she is not African American, Reno cannot project her own "image" onto the items. Rather, Reno approaches black memorabilia as, first, a knowledgeable collector, and second, as an investor. But she is also an educator whose *Encyclopedia* includes historical information about racism as well as price ranges for memorabilia items. In order to understand your collection, she reasons, you must understand each

According to Julian Bond, Chairman of the NAACP and a collector himself, ownership of racist memorabilia by African Americans today alters the original meaning of such objects. Item #A0613, Emergence of Advertising in America, 2000, Rare Book, Manuscript, and Special Collections Library, Duke University.

item's history. For Reno, the black memorabilia collection serves a pedagogical purpose.

Jan Lindenberger's explanation of the current trend in black memorabilia collecting is more race-specific. "It seems African American collectors are the people searching them out," she says in the preface to *More Black Memorabilia: A Handbook with Prices*. "Why would they collect items that are stereotypical and derogatory?" Lindenberger, who is not African American, asks, anticipating her audience's curiosity. She quotes an African American collector for the answer: "African Americans want to show their children how other races viewed them, and how times and attitudes have changed." She explains African American collecting as distinctive to *them* as a group.[5]

Julian Bond and the two white collectors agree on an important point. Black memorabilia no longer signals an immediate connection to racism; these collections are history. Bond finds that the images "represent yesterday's promise partially fulfilled today, and hold a pledge that tomorrow will be better."[6] However, Bond's reference to "partially fulfilled" promises indicates the African American collector's position with regards to the racism embedded in the images. African American collectors locate themselves at a measured distance from the victimization that the objects represent.

The African American collector's class status as an individual with enough disposable income to invest in multiple items is evidence of his or her historical remove from the immediacy of and vulnerability to racism. Such violence is what happened, or perhaps even still sometimes happens, to *other* people. This distance, however, is not historical. Rather, it is both geographical and class-specific. I believe it is also premature and somewhat disingenuous. The disingenuousness of what I call the African American collector's "heritage-preservation narrative" is clearly evident in the title of the text for which Bond has written the introduction: the *Black Americana Price Guide* means that Bond's "heritage" has a dollar value. The apparent relation of capitalism to racism is not new, yet the African American collector's ownership of, and participation in, the proliferation of racism's symbolic icons is a puzzling new version of an old story.

At the armory I learned the recent history of African American collecting. Before Malinda Saunders coorganized the First Annual Black Collectibles Show in 1984, the Civil Rights movement had sought to remove racist representations of African Americans in the media. Protests about depictions of Aunt Jemima, Uncle Ben, and Sambo resulted in changed images and revised representations. Racist images were beginning to disappear.

It was at this time that antique dealers saw an explosion in demand for racist artifacts, and the prices for black images answered the market forces of supply and demand. When demand began to exceed supply, one African American antique dealer at the show told me, "Why should they [white people] have them?

The "black-child" image came into popular advertising use between 1889 and 1925, a time when advertisers were learning how best to manipulate consumers. Trade card, circa 1900 (left) and an advertisement from Puck *magazine in 1898 (right), both courtesy of the author.*

That's when I started collecting them for myself and other black people to buy." For African American collectors and dealers alike, it became important that racist images become the property of African Americans.

At the armory showcase, some important facts about the trade became abundantly clear. African Americans collect grotesque black memorabilia, as distinguished from historical artifacts and documents, for at least two reasons: first, because the racist representations properly belong to those who were victimized by the stereotypes and violence they represent, and second, so that white people will not be able to claim the racism—in some frighteningly nostalgic way—as their own.

However, there is a third reason why African Americans are collecting black memorabilia, and it is one to which no one at the Tenth Annual Black Memorabilia Showcase would admit. African Americans collect black memorabilia because the trade is lucrative. The objectives of historical preservation that Julian Bond described attempt to mask the obvious economic gains.

In the years since the armory showcase, I have struggled to understand the effects and purpose of collecting grotesque black memorabilia. The distinction between the grotesque and other forms of representation is important here, since the characteristics of the grotesque—the fat, red lips, exaggerated coloring, the curious violence toward children—mark the items as signs of excess that exceed any apparent attempt toward realistic representation. Grotesque items also display instances in which body parts and physical characteristics are exaggerated to stand seemingly "in isolation and display."[7] The exaggerated skin color of my photocopies serves to emphasize the difference between white and black. Moreover, the brutality of those images positions the spectator as eyewitness to a crime, the narrative for which is urgent and necessary. For without an immediate explanatory narrative, the violence embodied in the object can be mistakenly attributed to the collector—and not to history.

It is just this violence that makes some collectors eschew the grotesque items of black memorabilia. In a *Detroit News* article, Michael Sharp, an African American collector based in Washington, D.C., says that, while he understands the need to preserve and even collect such memorabilia, as a collector he avoids buying these items: "I tend to stay away from those pieces that are real demeaning." Quoted in the same article, Malinda Saunders counters his resistance: "This is *our* history and *our* culture. This is nothing we did to ourselves; just how we were depicted" (my emphasis).[8] Again, in Saunders's view, how *we* "were depicted" belongs to *us*.

The grotesque is the rightful property of those whose representation was manipulated and exaggerated. Exactly how and why African American collectors claim ownership of these grotesque and racist images could be revealed by the price tags on the items in question. That is, although many collectors reject the

In Spike Lee's movie Bamboozled, Pierre Delecroix is troubled by his collection of memorabilia. The final scenes show him destroying the expensive collectibles. From Bamboozled, *courtesy of Photofest.*

grotesque objects, the multiple and various examples for sale at the showcase prove that they are widely regarded as important parts of the collecting enterprise for African Americans. Mr. Sharp is in the minority.

The African American collector's heritage-preservation narrative attempts to explain the violence as belonging to black history, yet its ostensibly historical orientation (it is "our heritage") never fully replaces the collected object's earlier racist narrative, which properly belongs to white supremacy. For the object's earlier narrative helped the dominant culture to understand its own racial identity by projecting opposite and distorted characteristics onto consumer goods, and then to exploit those characteristics to target consumption of specific products.

What I call the "black-child" image emerged in print advertising as a vehicle for the "new rhetorical imperative" of a post-Civil War new society. Like all the ads of the period, the images were designed for a "persuasive, imperative, and knowing" public sensibility. There were more goods available and more competition. Especially in regards to household items, manufacturers sought to persuade consumers to buy their products within the contexts of increased disposable income at the dawn of the industrial era.

In the historical development of modern advertising, the blackened caricatures appeared from 1889–1925, an era in which ads created consumer desires, and for this reason the black-child images I collected were not so much informative as symbolic.[9]

The symbolic function of the black-child image in advertising is considered a historically racist infantilization of blacks generally. Such advertisements represent a particularly racist historical perception, or stereotype, in which "the black" was constructed in advertising's field of desire as "the eternal child [or] the eternal dependent."[10] Black-child images serve early advertising's persuasive objectives, exaggerating a character's blackness for contrast to emphasize the quality of a particular cleaning product. Or the image's blackness proved the indelibility of a particular dye. The black-child image links blackness to domestic labor or to the victims in scenes of apparently comedic violence. Yet the humor of such images can only be understood if the viewer understands and accepts blackness as a symbolic outlet for aggression.

Early print advertising used the black-child image in so many symbolic scenes of race, violence, and labor that the characters' apparent identification as children is lost beneath the puzzling associations with multiple domestic products, from dye to shoes to soap. Such images become icons of a racist imagination that manipulates consumer behavior and produces desires not necessarily for black children but for specific brand names and products.

For African American collectors, such objects currently function in ironically similar ways as they enable new desires and new narratives in which the collectors are the storytellers who stand a measured distance from racist victimization.

SAY SAMBO, HO! WHERE IS YOUR SHOE?
THOSE CHEAP CUT NAILS WILL NEVER DO,
TIS HARD TO BEAT A HORSE WELL SHOD,
WITH PUTNAM NAILS FORGED FROM THE ROD.

Racist memorabilia also manifests the bourgeois African American collector's desire for a presegregation black identity and community. That is, Julian Bond and Malinda Saunders can only say "we" and "our" in the contexts of a collective and victimized past that, they insist, can be claimed through ownership of the racist and grotesque artifacts.

However, ownership of a victimized black identity as it is manifest in the African American collector's heritage-preservation narrative does not sever the connection between the object and its origin in white supremacy and racism. Racist icons tell the story of the violent creation of the "nigger," which was entirely uninterested in African American heritage or culture. Rather, the nigger emerges as the clearest evidence that African American culture is absent from black memorabilia's racist iconography and perpetuation of white-supremacist culture and identity.

Yet African American collectors gather, manipulate, and organize individual items in their collections, and therefore necessarily generate narratives of justification and explanation. Black memorabilia, like those objects in any collection, have individual stories and meanings. Each item of a collection is placed in relation to the other items, all of which together constitute the collection's unified and larger story of the collector's "interior self."[11] The chain of stories that are embedded in the black-child images I photocopied and the few I bought at the Silver Spring showcase illustrate how grotesque black memorabilia must always deal with narratives that African American collectors cannot control. For the larger story of grotesque artifacts is that which belongs to the racist imagination. In *Bamboozled* the racist artifacts of black memorabilia become symbolic of the differences between the privileged class of African Americans who collect such images and the street-level gangsta rap culture that recognizes that the images still resonate a hatred that their market value cannot hide.

Moreover, black-child images are among the most provocative primarily because they so often depict scenes of physical violence. For instance, the *Price Guide* offers a trading card from the late 1890s that depicts a violent kick given by a white clown to the backside of a black shoeshine boy—for no apparent reason. Another item for sale, an ink blotter whose screaming child advertises "Eagle Shirts," depicts an abandoned, horrified child hanging precariously from a tree limb by his ragged shirt. The relationship between product and image is currently elusive, yet the obviously racist violence overtakes its significance for black heritage or the effort to replace that violence with its cash value as an object. Both

opposite:

Can African American collectors' views of memorabilia supplant the intent of the objects' original creators?
Item #D0269 (above) and Item #A0164 (below), Emergence of Advertising in America, 2000, Rare Book,
Manuscript, and Special Collections Library, Duke University.

of these items appear in the *Price Guide*, and both are valuable additions to a collection of black memorabilia.

Whatever the objectives of African American collectors in their efforts to claim racist images, these historical images are not as easily defused or manipulated as collectors believe them to be. That is, African American collectors of black memorabilia explain their collections by identifying their possessions as part of a historical and political sea change in race relations in the United States. Yet the irony of black collectibles produces not so much a change in thinking as a recycling of old views. What I call "paradigm recycling" is the embrace of such items as artifacts of African American culture, or the heritage-preservation narrative. In *Bamboozled* the heritage-preservation narrative of black memorabilia fails to reassure by reminding Delecroix of the past; instead, the grotesque collection's items menacingly haunt him in his office. Delecroix then tries to destroy them in the film's final moments by smashing the priceless objects.

Yet, as heritage preservation, such narratives are essential to the habit of collecting. Cultural critic Susan Stewart's theories explain how each image or object in a collection requires a story, or narrative, that connects the object to its possessor. The narrative places each object in a chain of objects, which together constitute the collection. However, in order for the object to become a story of African American heritage, the current narrative must be taken from its story of white racism. As Stewart explains, "to construct the [collector's] narrative, it is necessary to obliterate the object's contexts of origin."[12]

Julian Bond's narrative positions the African American collector as the producer of his or her own history, which becomes possible by substituting the earlier narrative with another. Such substitution is a fantasy of manipulation as the African American collector, in the process of assembling racist artifacts, becomes "not simply the consumer of objects, [but] a producer of those objects, a producer by arrangement and manipulation" of the collection.[13] African American collectors reproduce white racism's violence when they assemble collections of grotesque black memorabilia. Yet the ethnic or racial identity of the collector does not obliterate the obvious violence of these figures. Rather, the acquisition and arrangement of a black memorabilia collection are the conditions under which the racist narrative reasserts itself as the primary story of the objects. The African American collector's heritage-preservation narrative cannot obliterate white racist identification because the object would then become meaningless.

The heritage-preservation narrative cannot control all the narratives that the images make possible. Nor can it claim to represent the sole meaning of these images primarily because the violent narratives of racism are still in circulation as lived experiences.

The African American collector's desire to locate black heritage in black memorabilia is a form of nostalgia indulged in by the privileged class behind which

RICE'S SEEDS.

A COTTON BALL.

Do you have occasion to
PURCHASE SEEDS
→ IF SO ←
RICE'S SEEDS ARE THE BEST
BECAUSE THEY ARE NORTHERN GROWN.
OVER.

The trading of this memorabilia by contemporary wealthy African Americans is one of the latest in a long series of complex connections between racism and capitalism in America. Item #A0460, *Emergence of Advertising in America*, 2000, Rare Book, Manuscript, and Special Collections Library, Duke University.

they hide purely capitalist drives. Racist artifacts are certainly historical, but their current value for African Americans indicates the extent to which urban, economically privileged blacks feel themselves disconnected from the current discrimination and violence experienced by less privileged African Americans. For ultimately the most important role of black memorabilia is to provide a fantasy of black community in the racism of historical icons. In addition, black memorabilia serves to increase class-consciousness among bourgeois African American collectors.

The trade has been aggressively wrested from white collectors as an effort to control the reading and interpretation of racist history—and to control a curiously race-specific flow of capital. Malinda Saunders reveals the relation of profit to heritage in startling terms: "Many white collectors have long appreciated and profited from selling and buying black memorabilia. So it's about time that black dealers and collectors profit from their own heritage."[14] African American collectors still utilize enormous amounts of disposable income to "profit" from the labor of black memorabilia. Among their gains is distance from the immediate, direct experiences of poverty and racist violence that the images represent.

The distancing African American collectors experience from the blatant racism of the images is both produced and navigated by the flow of cash. The act of buying the grotesque items transforms them into "images of ourselves" and then ironically creates the intimacy of possession when the item is placed within the familiar confines of the home. The grotesque and racist icon is clasped in an intimate, domestic embrace. In this way it is clear that African American collectors desire both distance from, and intimacy with, the items whose violence and hatred still issue uncontrollably as narratives of the racist imagination.

In order to defuse that violence, African American collectors claim an ironic identification with the images, buy the images, and then assemble them like lost children—grouped and organized upon the playground of America's racist past. The collection is disciplined and lovingly controlled; objects are claimed and then renamed. Black Sambo becomes "our history," and the tortured black-child is named "our image." The consequence of such substitution is the confusion of history—not its preservation.

Preservation requires a museum where history becomes priceless, and painful memories and narratives are suspended behind glass—ostensibly beyond the reach of monetary exchange. When the intimate identification with the racist image is abruptly broken through sale, the heritage-preservation narrative is revealed as a smokescreen. If the items are "heritage," then that heritage is, by definition, priceless—and that heritage does not belong only to black America's painful memories. That violence belongs to its site of origin: America's historical and racist neuroses, for which there is no dollar value.

The trafficking in racist images only complicates the violent history of racism;

DANDY JIM.

"Maybe they're white America's heritage," says African American media consultant Keith Woods, "but they aren't mine. My people were never caricatures." Item #D0302, Emergence of Advertising in America, 2000, Rare Book, Manuscript, and Special Collections Library, Duke University.

it does not dispel it, nor can it revise or overwrite it. Trading in such images reveals a historical and fundamental relationship clearly understood as the exploitative linking of African Americans and the grotesque to generate the flow of capital. For as long as black memorabilia generates wealth, the artifacts will produce capital in ways reminiscent of the wealth produced by slavery. That such wealth falls into the hands of slaves' descendants in no way diminishes its relationship to racism.

Moreover, many African Americans and whites in the Deep South still consider the recycling of racist images a disturbing practice. "I wouldn't collect them because they make me feel uncomfortable, and I don't like the way they look," says Curtis Austin, an African American historian, professor, and native of Mississippi. Austin's discomfort issues from his intimate experience with the original contexts for the images. For Austin the images are not of the past, since they still appear in small stores near his hometown of Hattiesburg, Mississippi. Instead, they are "current representations of white racism" that overwhelm their circulation as African American "heritage." According to Austin, "There is no amount of money that could make me claim them as *my* image."[15]

Keith Woods, an African American media consultant and native of New Orleans who now lives in Tampa, Florida, does not see his "heritage" in black memorabilia either. "Maybe they're white America's heritage, but they aren't mine. My people were never caricatures." Woods believes that the original artifacts should be taken out of circulation and "put into a museum."[16] Yet even that gesture will not solve the problem of collecting black memorabilia. The problem with African Americans collecting these objects issues from a tangle of contradictions be-

For author Lynn Casmier-Paz, the original racist meaning of the memorabilia can never be completely replaced. Advertisement from Town and Country Magazine *in 1920.*

Julian Bond Responds

Coeditor Harry L. Watson asked Julian Bond, Chairman of the Board of the NAACP, for his thoughts on Lynn Casmier-Paz's article, and Dr. Bond was kind enough to reply.

In his introduction to the Black Americana Price Guide, *activist and NAACP Chair Julian Bond wrote: "For others . . . these artifacts summon up yesterday's world, but in our hands and homes they become reminders of a different sort. They speak of triumph and overcoming, and inform us that despite what others thought and believed, we were never what they suggest." Photograph courtesy of Julian Bond.*

Dear Professor Watson:

Thank you for sending me a copy of Dr. Casmier-Paz's article. We disagree.

She wrongly conflates the myriad motives of a multitude of collectors—negative nostalgia, a decorating impulse, profit, a sanitizing embrace, and more—into one, and in an attack on all, disparagingly describes all as bourgeois.

Her characterization of black memorabilia collectors desiring "a pre-segregation black identity and community" is both historically impossible and wrong.

She properly credits me with constructing my own narrative of these objects and then denies me that right, calling it a "fantasy."

I have been black for 61 years. I lived in segregation, and have no desire to return to it. I do not know anyone else who does. I have been the victim of racism in the past and present day—as have most black people.

These images remind me of what others believed of me in the past and too many believe now; that memory, I believe, makes me stronger.

It is a common phenomenon to deny victims their legitimate anger or the acts of exorcism they consider valid; I am surprised to see this tactic employed in your pages.

Best wishes,
Julian Bond

tween history, collective identity, power, and representation. The African American collector's heritage-preservation narrative is a powerful (and expensive) attempt to revise and control a violent legacy. Yet such control gives the bourgeois African American collector an artificial and premature sense that racist violence is a thing of the past. Moreover, black memorabilia is ultimately the representation and property of white racism and its history.

Over time, I lost my compulsion to gather the images of the black-child in antique advertisements. I remained unconvinced that such images belonged to my heritage, yet the appeal of the black-child images caused me to experience no small measure of guilty desire to possess and therefore protect them. I had been driven to gather them because I felt they were somehow lost and forgotten. That is, my gathering had been driven by a parent's longing to wrench the images from those for whom their value lay in their exchange. I had wanted to "free" them from circulation and tuck them safely between thin plastic sheets. In this sense, I understand the collector's desire to take these images of violence and dismantle them, much like the African American deconstruction of the term "nigger," in which the violence of the term is softened and used affectionately to identify fellow African Americans. As in the instance where "nigger" becomes "my niggah," black memorabilia becomes "our heritage" in a powerful urge to somehow come to terms with the repugnant signs and symbols of a racist projection and its desire to dehumanize Africa's children. But, as I discovered, the success of such revisionist gestures is impossible.

For these images were never mine, nor were they ever intended for me. Rather, they remain icons of racist desire and longing, and to trade in such images would be a failed effort to replace their origins in the racist imagination with a new orientation in black heritage. African American cultural heritage is not so impoverished that it needs to claim grotesque artifacts as its own. However, before my final turn away from the violence and racism of those images, I saw one more advertisement. Behind a sign reading "$45," a Florida antique shop's plastic "Black Ephemera" bin held a full-page original ad from *Town and Country* magazine, 1920. The ad angered and saddened me, and I stood looking at it a long time, thinking about the shamelessly lucrative circulation of the black-child image. That image of impishly playful children was the last item I sought to rescue from circulation. And now I have no idea where I put it.

NOTES

1. Spike Lee, writer and producer, *Bamboozled* (2000).

2. Julian Bond, "Introduction," *Black Americana Price Guide*, ed. Kyle Husfloen (Antique Trader Books, 1996), vi–ix.

3. *Ibid.*, vii.

4. Dawn Reno, ed., "Introduction," *The Encyclopedia of Black Collectibles* (Wallace-Homestead Book Company, 1996), xi–xii.

5. Jan Lindenberger, *More Black Memorabilia: A Handbook with Prices*, 2nd edition (Schiffer Publishing, 1999), 3, 4.

6. Bond, "Introduction," *Black Americana Price Guide*, ix.

7. Susan Stewart, *On Longing: Narratives of the Miniature, the Gigantic, the Souvenir, the Collection* (Duke University Press, 1994), 105.

8. Michelle Singletary, "Collectibles: Rich in History—and Value—Black Memorabilia is Popular," *Detroit News*, 30 December 1995 (www.detnews.com/menu/stories/30241.html).

9. Raymond Williams, "Advertising: The Magic System," *Problems in Materialism and Culture* (London: Verso Books, 1988), 172, 8; Malcolm Barnard, "Advertising: The Rhetorical Imperative," *Visual Culture*, ed. Chris Jenks (Routledge Press, 1995), 33; John Kenneth Galbraith, *The Affluent Society* (Houghton Mifflin, 1977), 145.

10. Jan Nederveen Pieterse, *White on Black: Images of Africans and Blacks in Western Popular Culture* (Yale University Press, 1992), 152.

11. Stewart, *On Longing*, 158.

12. *Ibid.*

13. *Ibid.*

14. Singletary, "Collectibles," 30 December 1995.

15. Interview with Curtis Austin, 5 August 2000.

16. Interview with Keith Woods, 5 October 2000.

My Twentieth Century
Leaves From a Journal

by Anne Firor Scott

Anne Firor Scott is W. K. Boyd Professor of History Emerita at Duke University. In 1970 her book The Southern Lady: From Pedestal to Politics, 1830–1930 *virtually established the modern study of southern wom-
en's history, and it has never gone out of print. Since then, Anne Scott has taught at Duke and all over the
world, inspiring legions of younger followers to insist on the importance of women in southern history. To
honor her eightieth birthday, the Schlesinger Library for the History of Women in America held a symposium
in 2001 in which a number of scholars paid tribute and Scott reflected on the highlights of her career. This
is what she said.*

I am not sure why the number eighty seems so weighty, compared
with its predecessor or even with its successor. What are the
landmark ages? Being old enough to drive? To vote? Or fifty?
One young friend told me gloomily that after fifty it is all down-
hill. I could only respond that my resumé *begins* at age fifty. At
any rate, eighty is a good time for putting the pieces together, for trying to make
sense of eight decades of life.

My title was inspired by the protagonist in Penelope Lively's novel *Moon Tiger*,
who says—apropos of her plan to write a history of the world—"My Victorians
are not your Victorians. My seventeenth century is not yours. The voice of . . .
Darwin, of whoever you like, speaks in one tone to me, in another to you. The
signals of my own past come from the received past. The lives of others slot into
my own life." Like this woman, I assume that my twentieth century is not yours
and that we can only imperfectly convey our individual life experience to each
other. But I also assume that with documents the historian can try to reconstruct
a partly shared past—and that we are all primary sources for the social historian.

The documents in this case are thirty-one volumes of a journal begun in the
summer of 1939. For the years before the journal I must rely on treacherous
memory.

My beginning was decidedly provincial and my geographic frame narrow. Born
in a village in southwest Georgia, I grew up from age two in the small, sleepy town
of Athens, Georgia, founded in the late eighteenth century to be the home of the
state university. When I enrolled there 150 years later, one member of the faculty
had taught my grandfather, and his colleagues were nearly all in a nineteenth-

century mold, more like Mr. Chips than like twentieth-century scholars. The most admired of them were classicists.

Retirement was not even a concept. There were no pensions. Faculty members continued to teach until illness or death brought their careers to an end. I am astonished to find myself in 1939 writing, "I enjoy him [the professor of Latin] immensely. But somehow I'm not sure he isn't a prisoner in the ivied walls of the University and the world at large is just a mass of shadows to him." It seems unlikely that I had at that point come upon Plato's cave, but whence came that echo?

Faculty people, along with impecunious members of long established families, a few lawyers, a couple of doctors, and a handful of prosperous businessmen made up the town elite. With few exceptions, these people lived in what was called genteel poverty. Across the river was the mill village about which children on our side of town, or indeed our elders, knew very little. Beyond the town limits were many farm families, mostly poor, and half the population of the county was black.

That vanished world, so clear in my mind's eye, is now totally gone. Soon there will be no one alive who remembers it.

How can I convey to you, who are mostly younger and mostly not southern, what it *felt* like? The drowsy summer atmosphere when few students were around, and when, in that dark age before air conditioning, everyone, perforce, moved slowly. High ceilings and electric fans helped for those who could afford them. Everyone else simply accepted being hot as a fact of life. Evenings found most

"Georgia had never recovered from the Depression of 1921, but 1929 certainly made things worse, as more banks failed, people were laid off, the university could not meet its payroll, and my grandfather's cotton business nearly went under." Anne Scott's father inspects an ear of corn at the market in downtown Athens (above) shortly after the depression of 1921, courtesy of the author. Athens in 1923 (below), courtesy of the Hargrett Rare Book and Manuscript Library, the University of Georgia.

folks on front porches, their own or those of their neighbors. Twice each day a dignified African American gentleman delivered the mail on foot—letters bearing a three-cent stamp and often with only the name of the town for an address. He knew every child by name.

Youngsters walked to school and in summer had to make their own recreation—in my case by hanging around the neighborhood tennis court and imitating what I saw. That tennis court was itself emblematic of life in the first part of this century: a great aunt had built it for her five children. Three of them died of tuberculosis in young adulthood, yet she continued all her life to maintain the court for all the other youngsters in the neighborhood, one of whom turned out to be some sort of state tennis champion.

An occasional summer visitor was a great event. When a visiting company brought us *Madame Butterfly*, it played in the university gym and provided my first encounter with opera and with Puccini. The village library, which had come into being thanks to the WPA, was in the building of a failed bank and was entirely composed of discards from the estates of old families or gifts from an occasional member of the Book of the Month Club.

In the 1930s another depression-born agency built an outdoor swimming pool

"Nothing as exciting as war had stirred the lethargy of an Athens summer for many years—and Poland was a long way off. . . . By then I was a junior at the university. . . . War brought change as people moved about in large numbers. Southern boys found themselves in India and Hawaii, Okinawa and Guam." The caption under this wartime photograph reads: "Problem for the Class of '42—Which Shall It Be, the Army, the Navy or Marines?" Anne Scott, photographed while at college, courtesy of the author. Wartime photograph courtesy of the Hargrett Rare Book and Manuscript Library, the University of Georgia.

for white kids that instantly became the center of our summer life. Black kids had only the muddy river. Model A Fords and various newer models had no trouble finding space downtown—parking meters were unknown. On Saturday afternoon, black and white farmers drove their wagons to town, stuffed with women and children, and for a few hours the sidewalks were filled, activity reigned. The county agricultural agent, one of the most important people in town, held office hours from two to five on Saturday.

Sunday was the quietest day of all. Everyone, or so it seemed, went to Sunday school and church, where ladies bore the heat with fans thoughtfully provided by the local undertaker. Occasional tent revivals brought large crowds to hear itinerant evangelists. Even the staid First Methodist Church had an annual revival, and one of our numerous cousins, a presiding elder in the church, was known for his "hellfire and damnation" sermons.

Most of the town lived in undistinguished houses built after 1865. Stately antebellum houses, mostly in bad repair, lined three streets. A few ancient, white-haired gentlemen with flowing mustaches, and their ladies in dotted Swiss dresses, matched the houses. Our house had been built in the 1850s, its foot-thick brick walls put in place by slaves. My father had bought it, along with two acres of land, dozens of bearing pecan trees, and a tumbledown garage, for six thousand dollars just before a bank failure swept away his savings.

In another part of town black families lived in small, often unpainted houses on rutted, unpaved streets. For them sanitation consisted of wells and outhouses. Black women washed white folks' clothes in iron pots filled by hand and set over a wood fire. Lacking electricity, washerwomen heated their irons on wood stoves that also served to cook their meals, winter and summer.

For my three young brothers and me, forays into a larger world took the form of occasional trips to Atlanta, which was, my father liked to say, sixty miles and a hundred years away. The great treat was lunch in the S & W cafeteria on Peachtree Street.

Georgia had never recovered from the depression of 1921, but 1929 certainly made things worse, as more banks failed, people were laid off, the university could not meet its payroll, and my grandfather's cotton business nearly went under. Thin-as-a-rail black boys, who had lugged golf clubs around the course for whatever small change the golfer had seen fit to hand them, knocked on our kitchen door for permission to pick up pecans from the numerous trees in our yard saying, "I ain't had nothing to eat all day, Miss."

In 1937 my father's World War I bonus enabled him to pay my forty-dollars-a-term tuition at the University of Georgia. Two years later—midsummer 1939—I began a journal: "to give me some idea where my college days are going. They pass so fast—then I can't remember what happened."

So journal keeping was already a daily habit when Hitler invaded Poland. Re-

"For a moment the world stopped turning [when Franklin Roosevelt died] while we, a great nation, felt ourselves suddenly headless, directionless." President Roosevelt, signing the declaration of war, courtesy of the Library of Congress's Farm Security Administration and Office of War Information Collection.

reading now, I recognize what we had been taught about the failings of the Versailles treaty and the deceitfulness of British propaganda. Do I hear the voice of Carlton J. Hayes, historian and diplomat, when I read, "England and France woefully point to Hitler as the 'sole cause' and completely neglect Monsieur Clemenceau and Mr. Lloyd George and the other gentlemen who framed the Treaty of Versailles. After all if they had been a little more humane Hitler might still be an Austrian house painter."

Along with comments about censorship—I assumed both sides were lying—and fears that the FBI would become like the Gestapo, I noted that townspeople were simultaneously horrified and exhilarated. Nothing as exciting as a war had stirred the lethargy of an Athens summer for many years—and Poland was a long way off. My notes reveal a stunningly self-assured adolescent, or—more charitably—a precocious young historian.

By then I was a junior at the university. The student body was mostly from small Georgia towns, though there were a few relative urbanites from Atlanta and Savannah. In retrospect, those destined for fame or fortune were as likely to come from tiny villages as from the occasional city.

Too impecunious to join a sorority, I compensated by striving to be a campus leader. In that capacity I took charge of two earnest and passionate young women

"The day after the President died my housemates and many of our friends sat in
Lafayette Square with a thousand silent mourners in a mood of enormous sadness."
F. D. R.'s funeral, courtesy of the Library of Congress.

who came to plead the cause of the Spanish Republicans. Excited by their stories, we gave them our nickels and dimes and felt ourselves taking part in the great world. If we were soon to exhibit ambivalence about the motives of England and France, in 1938 we had none about the Spanish Republicans. They were the inspiring Good Guys. From the perspective of sixty years I can see somewhat more complexity. Curiously, admiration for the Spanish Republicans did not prevent many of us from calling ourselves pacifists.

So it was that events, large and small, beyond the bounds of Georgia, and varieties of human behavior beyond the ken of my ever so respectable extended family, began to stretch my horizons.

WAR CHANGES AND SEA CHANGES

War brought change as people moved about in large numbers. Yankees showed up all over the South. Southern boys found themselves in India and Hawaii, Okinawa and Guam. (Eventually one of my brothers would be assigned by the U.S. Army to run the railroads in northern Kyushu—a place of whose existence I doubt any of us had known five years before.) I could paraphrase Henry Adams: the Georgia farmer of 1939—most Georgians *were* farmers in that year—was closer to his forefather of 1839 than to his successor of 1946.

Looking back, it is clear that I was living on more than one level at the same time. Much of my journal has a dismal, apocalyptic tone. For example, at the end of the terrible summer of 1940, a long reflection on the first year of war ends with "It seems that our generation has grown up into a world of horror." After Pearl Harbor such entries multiplied, as did expressions of guilt that I was not suffering while my male friends were more and more going into combat. My freshman true love (who had later married my best friend) died in the first months of the Pacific War. Long essays focused on this and other horrors would continue through the war. A typical one was written during the Battle of the Bulge: "The saddest Christmas that I can remember. . . . Suddenly hopes for the future seem to dim and vanish like the misty clouds on a winter night . . . the prospect of a world without young men becomes a grim possibility. And if we kill off our brains and talent, for what have we fought?"

Yet through all the years from 1939 to the summer of 1945, it is clear that no matter how bad things seemed in the great world, in the small one normal young adult life went on. Young men came and went, romances blossomed and foundered, and, as it turned out, for me and for many others it was a great time to be an ambitious young woman. As men went to war, one door after another opened to women. Graduate fellowships, Washington internships—jobs normally reserved for men—came my way. New experiences multiplied. There was so much going on, so much to learn. The journal alternated between despair and exuberance.

By the summer of 1943, I was in Washington—in what was then called the center of the free world. A few months working for an inspiring Congressman misled me into thinking that I understood the workings of the United States government. A job in the national office of the League of Women Voters introduced me to still-powerful, aging suffragists and through them to the long history of American women. The league was then only twenty-two years old and well aware of its suffrage origins.

At the same time, the league brought me in touch with numerous contemporary women who were movers and shakers in their communities. Some of their collective achievements were extraordinary: rewriting city charters, revising state constitutions, uncovering misuse of public funds, supporting taxes about which their businessmen husbands were often dubious. People see what they are prepared to see, and all unknown to me at the time, these women were teaching me to see things that other historians had overlooked.

My job had other consequences: my parents had never suggested that being female should limit my aspirations, and the League of Women Voters and all the other women's associations with which it cooperated reinforced this assumption.

"Two years after the war ended, I married a returned Navy pilot [Andrew Scott] and with him joined the mass of GI Bill students at Harvard. For two years I forgot about writing a journal." Photographs courtesy of the author.

Daily my world expanded as I tried to make sense of Congress, the bureaucracy, of Washington—a segregated city operating as the center of the fight for world freedom—and other paradoxes. I began to have friends from all points of the compass; some very adventurous ones made me feel a timid soul. At first I was in awe of the Ivy League and Seven Sisters graduates among them, but in time they seemed not so very different from me. When I had time I worried about the future: what career of all those that increasingly seemed possible should I choose?

I often felt painfully ignorant and thought if I could just study more, learn more, the seemingly intractable problems surrounding us might prove soluble. Our apartment was just two blocks from a branch library, and night after night I combed the shelves hoping for light and wisdom. My journal is filled with anxious questions. I cringe a little as I read much earnest commentary. A typical example grew out of an assignment the Congressman had given me that led me to understand that when he depended on historical analogies in his ardent opposition to monopolies and cartels, he really did not know what he was talking about. I wrote with portentous solemnity: "I am impressed with the difficulty involved in making accurate statements. It is necessary to check information that comes via hearsay, books, magazines or newspaper by talking to someone who is working with the subject. Even then the great danger is that false conclusions will result from having access to only part of the truth." And later: "How small an aspect of reality can be seen from a single standpoint . . . our American 'approach to life' is but one of many."

On one level, the immense suffering around the world weighed heavily on noncombatants like myself and led to moments of despair. On another, it was a happy and exhilarating time for me and other young women like me.

Franklin Roosevelt's death was certainly a moment of despair. I tried to capture the experience: "For a moment the world stopped turning while we, a great nation, felt ourselves suddenly headless, directionless. The pilot gone and the ship moving rapidly to port—the port where all our problems are scattered over the dock." (Years later I found that Dean Acheson, one of my heroes, had written in *his* journal: "One felt as though the city had vanished leaving its inhabitants to wander about bewildered looking for a familiar landmark. The dominant emotion was not sorrow so much as apprehension at finding oneself alone and lost . . . the familiar had given way to an ominous unknown.") Perhaps it was a metaphor for the double life so many of us were living that the day after the president died my housemates and many of our friends sat in Lafayette Square with a thousand silent mourners in a mood of enormous sadness. The whole city of Washington was quiet that day—even on the streetcars nobody talked. Yet on the day of the funeral, with all work suspended, we happily paddled canoes on the Potomac.

Then, Hiroshima. My four-woman household dubbed ourselves the Ten Years to Live Club—and three of us responded by getting married or taking off for graduate school. I stayed on trying to explain the implications of atomic energy to far-flung members of the League of Women Voters. It appalls me to realize how little I understood the complexity of the issues—and with what confidence I wrote!

Two years after the war ended, I married Andrew Scott, a returned Navy pilot, and with him joined the mass of GI Bill students at Harvard. Cambridge in 1947 would be more easily recognized by students of the 1920s than by those present today, but for me it was a journey into hitherto unimagined sophistication. Faculty and students alike seemed so learned, so well read, so cosmopolitan—would one ever be like that? And for some reason (shock of the new? who knows) for two years I forgot about writing a journal. Memory says it was a wonderful time—an expanding two years punctuated by horrendous events such as the invasion of Czechoslovakia or the Berlin blockade.

It was during this unrecorded time that I first encountered the Women's Archives (forerunner of the Schlesinger Library). It was then a locked room in the basement of Byerly Hall. One could get the key, dust off a table, use the collections, and lock the door again. I may have been the only user in 1948—who could have dreamed of the five thousand or more who come now each year?

My journal came back to life just after I passed my general exam with something less than flying colors and my husband was finishing his dissertation. We were on our way back to Washington where the Cold War loomed. It was a sign of the times that, when a close friend came for dinner as we prepared to leave Cambridge, he and Andrew were deeply engaged in discussing the best way to transport explosives to enemy countries.

Once settled in Washington I began a daily trek to the Library of Congress,

"Somehow, that Fall [1948], I found my way to the historic meeting of the Southern Historical Association in Williamsburg—historic because Vann Woodward and a few others had, so to say, smuggled John Hope Franklin in to give a paper and attend the dinner, which had never before included a black scholar." John Hope Franklin, photographed by Les Todd, courtesy of Duke University Photography.

struggling to make myself into a serious historian. The city, I wrote, is "much the same as always. Full of politics and bureaucrats and people who try to influence them . . . all the people at parties are bright young bureaucrats of this or that agency—talking shop."

Somehow, that fall, I found my way to the historic meeting of the Southern Historical Association in Williamsburg—historic because Vann Woodward and a few others had, so to say, smuggled John Hope Franklin in to give a paper and attend the dinner, which had never before included a black scholar. Though I would not have thought so at the time, perhaps that trip marked the beginning of a career, for it was there that I first met not only Woodward but also David Potter, both of whom would, years later, give me crucial support.

But that day was far in the future. Home from Williamsburg I discovered that I was pregnant. The library staff joked about the prospect of a baby born in the midst of the manuscripts. It didn't happen, but we might speculate about prenatal influences since today Rebecca Scott confesses to loving archives, almost wherever found.

The invasion of South Korea shook our world. Intelligence reports to which Andrew was privy indicated that the war might widen, that Washington might be bombed. Rather precipitately he put me on a train for Georgia. I was instructed not to say anything about the alarming intelligence that had brought me home. What could I tell all those solicitous family members about my unexpected ar-

"Intelligence reports to which Andrew was privy indicated that the [Korean] war might widen, that Washington might be bombed. Rather precipitately he put me on a train for Georgia. I was instructed not to say anything about the alarming intelligence that had brought me home. What could I tell all those solicitous family members about my unexpected arrival so close to the baby's due date? In deepest confidence I consulted my father. Oh, he said, there is no problem. Just say you didn't want the baby to be born up North. He was right. No one batted an eye." Photograph courtesy of the author.

rival so close to the baby's due date? In deepest confidence I consulted my father. Oh, he said, there is no problem. Just say you didn't want the baby to be born up north. He was right. No one batted an eye. It was a perfectly acceptable explanation for my sudden appearance, as it happened, three days before Rebecca decided to arrive and bring with her, of course, the intimidating new experience of parenthood.

For a few years, my world seemed to be closing in as I adjusted to new limitations. When Andrew flew off to France to help the Foreign Aid Agency begin to unify Western Europe, I stayed home, chasing a two year old. My old friends at the League of Women Voters saved me with a part-time job, but the dissertation, ah where was it? Castigating myself for sloth became a recurrent theme of the journal. When the Republicans took over in 1952 we left Washington for academia. In the ensuing two years babies number two and three, arriving only sixteen months apart, brought the dissertation to a complete halt. In the small Quaker community of Haverford College, daily life took all my time.

Then came one of those critical moments. I had hardly been out of the house for weeks; one or the other of the young ones always had a cold, and we had almost no money for household help. Feeling sorry for me, Andrew came home one afternoon saying that one of his colleagues, a historian, would be that night talking about his research. He suggested that I put on my snow boots and go. I did. Wallace MacCaffrey was so eloquent, so passionate, about Elizabethan England that in a curious way he roused me to shake off my scholarly lethargy, to apply for a fellowship, to go to work and finish what I routinely called the "damned dissertation." Eighteen months later I had the elusive Ph.D.

That, in some sense, made all else possible. Most immediately it made possible a chance to teach American history at Haverford College and to discover my true métier. I walked into that first class to face thirty young men who had thought they were registering for a gut course. One of them later told me with considerable feeling that the first exam changed their expectations, especially the question "Which way was the wind blowing in the Caribbean on October 11, 1492, and why does it matter." For me, and I believe for them, life became more challenging, complicated, and interesting as we tried together to understand something about the American past.

I have done many things in a by now long life, but outside of family nothing has given me more true and lasting pleasure than teaching. Students have been my teachers in many ways. Long reflections on teaching are an important part of my journal: how to do it, what it should be accomplishing, how to understand the immense variety of young people who turned up in class. Over and over I dissected particular classes, always vowing to do it better next time.

In rereading the journal, I detect three sea changes in the times and the life the journal chronicles. The successive wars of the twentieth century and my caution-

"Living in the Quaker community of Haverford College, daily life took all my time." Anne Scott with her children in Haverford, courtesy of the author.

ary responses to the risks of war recur in this journal of sixty years. Second, the rising tide of options for women was my lived experience and a remarkable gift for me as for my daughter, and I trust for my granddaughters after me. And, as visible in retrospect as either of these, was a third sea change of the century: the Civil Rights movement, to which I awakened slowly and in which I became involved, at first hesitantly and later as a compelling cause.

Raised in the Jim Crow South, living with black people, I had been slow to recognize the meaning of race, of the colossal failure of myself and my fellow countrymen and women to live up to principles of freedom and justice for our black citizens. Slowly, beginning in the early 1940s, I had begun to think about the question. I can mark one moment in the 1950s when the word "discrimination" suddenly took on great meaning.

We were living in Haverford. The husband of my children's beloved Nanny, a black man from North Carolina, lost his job. In all ignorance and innocence I said cheerfully, "Let's get the help wanted ads and make a list for you." We sat down together with the classifieds. Who knows what was in his mind, but as we went through the ads I became steadily more embarrassed. It was clear that almost none of the jobs advertised would be open to a man of his color—this in Philadelphia, the City of Brotherly Love.

Soon the Montgomery bus boycott riveted our attention, and by the time we got to Chapel Hill in 1958 things were heating up there. In short order I found my timorous self knocking on doors asking sometimes quite hostile people to sign a

petition asking that our children's school admit one black student whose parents had applied for transfer. Somehow, held to the course by a dedicated neighbor, I learned to accept the hostility and keep going. I was dismayed when the school board turned down our petition. How could they not *see*, I kept asking—quite forgetting my own years of blindness. Reflecting on the experience in my journal I spoke of how courage grows with each step, and "next time I would know much better how to do it."

From that point forward "the race question," as it was called, became a recurrent theme for contemplation and then for my writing and teaching. I noticed things that had doubtless been there, unperceived, all my life. A typical entry from the sixties reads, "In years to come 1963 may have a place in the history books along with 1776 and 1860—in retrospect it will possibly be the year the American Negro decided he had had enough. It is interesting to speculate as to what the state of American society would be now if the voice of the advanced liberals had been heeded in 1910, if education and integrated housing had been available."

Of the numerous eye-opening experiences of the sixties, one of the most concentrated was a week spent as a volunteer with the first summer of Head Start. Judging by the space devoted to that week, it was a time when my learning curve

"The unexamined life is not worth living—and this record provides the raw material for such examination. Was it worth the thousands of hours I have spent making this record and the narcissistic effort to make sure it is preserved for an unknown posterity? Rereading my lived experience has become a means of understanding it." Anne Scott, courtesy of the author.

went straight up. Among many other things, I wrote about the partial awakening of a teacher who had taken the job because it paid well and who began with the assumption that black children were inherently slow. I noted the day she said with amazement, "Some of these children are really bright!"

It must have been at about this time that the president of the black student group at Duke showed up in my survey course, which led me to reorganize the syllabus to look at the American past from the perspective of African Americans. I'm not sure how that black student viewed the course, but the white students found it exhilarating. This was not the familiar old movie they had feared; they wrote their primary source papers with astounding diligence. My most recent pedagogical experiment was a course called "Parallel Lives: Black and White Women in American History," which I taught at the University of Mississippi in a class made up of equal numbers of black and white students. I have found a focus for my ninth decade.

So what does this excursion into the past tell me?

The journal now encompasses thirty-one volumes and a number of odd bits. It is deposited among rare books and manuscripts at Duke, and a microfilm of it is at Schlesinger—both under seal for twenty-five years after my death—a provision to allow total candor. Whatever I thought in early years, by the 1950s I already saw myself as making a record for some future historian. So there is my life, written for years in longhand, then on typewriter, and finally on computer, filling several thousand pages. Without it much would be lost forever, or remembered only with the modifications that new experience imposes on memory.

We have it on classical authority that the unexamined life is not worth living—and this record provides the raw material for such examination. Was it worth the thousands of hours I have spent making this record and the narcissistic effort to make sure it is preserved for an unknown posterity? Rereading my lived experience has become a means to understanding it. Perhaps some future historians will find that experience useful. At any rate, I wish them in advance bon voyage as they marry my attempt at insight with their views in hindsight.

Audubon Drive, Memphis

POETRY BY JIM SEAY

From Jailhouse Rock ©*1957 by Loew's Incorporated, Avon Productions, and M-G-M.*
Courtesy of the Museum of Modern Art Film Stills Archive.

There's a black-and-white photo of Elvis
and his father Vernon in their first swimming pool.
Elvis is about twenty-one and "Heartbreak Hotel"
has just sold a million.
When he bought the house,
mainly for his mother Gladys they say,
it didn't have a pool,
so this is new.
The water is up to the legs of Vernon's trunks
and rising slowly as he stands there
at attention almost.
Elvis is sitting or kneeling on the bottom,
water nearly to his shoulders,
his face as blank and white
as the five feet of empty poolside at his back.

The two of them are looking at the other side
of the pool and waiting for it to fill.
In the book somewhere
it says the water pump is broken.
The garden hose a cousin found is not in the frame,
but that's where the water is coming from.
In the background over Vernon's head you can see
about three stalks of corn
against white pickets in a small garden
I guess Gladys planted.
You could press a point and say that in the corn
and the fence, the invisible country
cousin and mother, the looks on Elvis's and Vernon's
faces, the partly filled pool, we can read
their lives together, the land
they came from, the homage they first thought
they owed the wealth beginning to accumulate,
the corny songs and films,
and that would be close but not quite central.
Closer than that is the lack
of anything waiting in the pool we'd be
prompted to call legend
if we didn't know otherwise.
They're simply son and father wondering if it's true
they don't have to drive a truck
tomorrow for a living.
But that's not it either.
What it reduces to is the fact that most of us
know more or less everything
that is happening to them
as though it were a critical text
embracing even us and our half-mawkish
geographies of two or three word obituaries:
in the case of Kennedy, for example, I was walking
across a quad in Oxford,
Mississippi; King's death too caught me in motion,
drifting through dogwood in the Shenandoah.
As for Elvis,
there were some of us parked outside a gas station
just over the bridge from Pawley's Island
with the radio on.

That's enough.
I know the differences.
But don't think they're outright.
The photo is 1034 Audubon Drive, Memphis,
and then it's Hollywood,
still waiting for the pool to fill.

Reprinted by permission of Louisiana State University Press from *Open Field, Understory: New and Selected Poems*, by James Seay. Copyright 1997 by James Seay.

Up Beat Down South

"The Death of Emma Hartsell"

BY BRUCE E. BAKER

In the mid-1960s, J. E. Mainer became the first person to record "The Death of Emma Hartsell," and in 1967 he published a songbook that included "Song of Emma Hartsell," which he claimed to have written. J. E. Mainer with his Mountaineers, courtesy of the Southern Folklife Collection, Wilson Library, the University of North Carolina at Chapel Hill.

"In eighteen-hundred and ninety-eight," as the song tells us, "Sweet Emma met with an awful fate." Sweet Emma was Emma Hartsell, the twelve-year-old daughter of a farmer in Cabarrus County, North Carolina, and the awful fate she met was murder. Just as awful, though, was the fate met by Tom Johnson and Joe Kizer a few hours later, hanged from a dogwood tree by a mob just outside of the town of Concord. Johnson and Kizer were black, Hartsell was white, and "The Death of Emma Hartsell" is a ballad that reminded everyone who heard it, mostly white folks, of just what that meant in 1898 in North Carolina.

Lots of North Carolinians met awful fates in 1898. Tempers ran high. One-party rule had been upset for four years in North Carolina as Republicans joined forces with Populists in a fusion coalition that gained control first of the legislature and then of the governor's office. White Democrats decided to take back control. To do so, they had to convince the white farmers in the Populist party to break ranks with the Republicans, whose strength lay in the support of the vast majority of the state's black voters and a fair number of whites, especially in the mountains. The strategy Democratic leaders—especially Charles B. Aycock, Josephus Daniels, and Furnifold Simmons—hit upon was to inspire fear. To frighten African Americans away from the polls, they brought in Senator "Pitchfork" Ben Tillman from neighboring South Carolina to instruct local Democratic clubs on the finer points of terrorism. To keep whites in line, they whipped up racial fears and animosities that had briefly been submerged. Daniels's newspaper, the Raleigh *News and Observer*, manufactured and circulated stories of unspeakable outrages committed by black men on white women.

It was in this climate that Emma Hartsell's parents went off to church one Sunday morning at the end of May. Emma stayed home to look after a younger sister who was ill. Her parents returned to find her dead on the kitchen floor. A search was made, and Johnson and Kizer were carried to the jail in Concord. Later that evening, a mob broke into jail, carried the men to Big Cold Water Hill outside of town, and dragged them up. No one was punished for the lynching. Soon afterwards, a woman named Mary Baker wrote a poem, ten verses that told the story of Emma and Tom and Joe and the mob. A little later, some singer picked up the poem, added a final verse, and set it to a tune used for "Barbara Allen." The song was widely known in the North Carolina Piedmont northeast of Charlotte. Folklorists collected it from schoolchildren in the 1920s, and the story, usually with the ballad, was a regular item in newspaper feature columns for decades.

"THE DEATH OF EMMA HARTSELL"

In eighteen hundred and ninety-eight,
Sweet Emma met with an awful fate;
'Twas on the holy Sabbath day
When her sweet life was snatched away.

It set my brain all in a whirl
To think of that poor little girl,
Who rose that morning fair and bright,
And before five was a mangled sight.

It caused many a heart to bleed
To think and hear of such deed.
Her friends, they shed many a tear.
Her throat was cut from ear to ear.

Just as the wind did cease to blow,
They caught the men, 'twas Tom and Joe.
The sheriff he drove in such a dash
The howling mob could scarcely pass.

They got to town by half past seven.
Their necks were broken before eleven.
The people there were a sight to see.
They hung them to a dogwood tree.

Fathers and mothers a warning take—
Never leave your children for God's sake.
But take them with you wherever you go
And always think of Tom and Joe.

Kind friends, we all must bear in mind
They caught the men who did the crime.
There's not a doubt around the lurk,
Tom said he held her while Joe did the work.

Sweet Emma has gone to a world of love
Where Tom and Joe dare not to go.
We think they've gone to hell below
For treating poor little Emma so.

Dear friends, we all remember this,
That Emma will be sadly missed.
And one thing more I also know—
This world is rid of Tom and Joe.

As they stood on death's cold brink
Joe Kizer begged the man for drink.
No drink, no drink, the man replied.
To Hell, to Hell your soul must fly.

INDIVIDUAL *subscription request*

Please enter my subscription to *Southern Cultures* at the rate of $28 for four quarterly issues [Add $12 for postage outside the US.] *This price is good until December 31, 2003*

❑ My check or money order, payable to THE UNIVERSITY OF NORTH CAROLINA PRESS, is enclosed in an envelope with this card.

❑ Please charge my Visa or MasterCard [circle one].

CARD NUMBER _____ EXP. DATE _____

SIGNATURE _____ DAYTIME PHONE _____

NAME _____

ADDRESS _____

_____ ZIP CODE _____

Southern cultures

For fastest service, please call [919] 966-3561, ext. 256, Monday–Friday between 9:30 a.m. and 4:00 p.m. EST with credit card information or fax your order to [800] 272-6817. You can also send e-mail to uncpress_journals@unc.edu.

INDIVIDUAL *subscription request*

Please enter my subscription to *Southern Cultures* at the rate of $28 for four quarterly issues [Add $12 for postage outside the US.] *This price is good until December 31, 2003*

❑ My check or money order, payable to THE UNIVERSITY OF NORTH CAROLINA PRESS, is enclosed in an envelope with this card.

❑ Please charge my Visa or MasterCard [circle one].

CARD NUMBER _____ EXP. DATE _____

SIGNATURE _____ DAYTIME PHONE _____

NAME _____

ADDRESS _____

_____ ZIP CODE _____

INDIVIDUAL *subscription request*

Please enter my subscription to *Southern Cultures* at the rate of $28 for four quarterly issues [Add $12 for postage outside the US.] *This price is good until December 31, 2003*

❑ My check or money order, payable to THE UNIVERSITY OF NORTH CAROLINA PRESS, is enclosed in an envelope with this card.

❑ Please charge my Visa or MasterCard [circle one].

CARD NUMBER _____ EXP. DATE _____

SIGNATURE _____ DAYTIME PHONE _____

NAME _____

ADDRESS _____

_____ ZIP CODE _____

**NO POSTAGE
NECESSARY IF
MAILED
IN THE
UNITED STATES**

BUSINESS REPLY MAIL

FIRST CLASS MAIL   PERMIT NO. 509   CHAPEL HILL, NC

Postage will be paid by addressee:

The University of North Carolina Press
Journals Fulfillment
Post Office Box 2288
Chapel Hill, NC 27515-2288

**NO POSTAGE
NECESSARY IF
MAILED
IN THE
UNITED STATES**

BUSINESS REPLY MAIL

FIRST CLASS MAIL   PERMIT NO. 509   CHAPEL HILL, NC

Postage will be paid by addressee:

The University of North Carolina Press
Journals Fulfillment
Post Office Box 2288
Chapel Hill, NC 27515-2288

**NO POSTAGE
NECESSARY IF
MAILED
IN THE
UNITED STATES**

BUSINESS REPLY MAIL

FIRST CLASS MAIL   PERMIT NO. 509   CHAPEL HILL, NC

Postage will be paid by addressee:

The University of North Carolina Press
Journals Fulfillment
Post Office Box 2288
Chapel Hill, NC 27515-2288

Democratic leaders—especially Josephus Daniels (left), Charles B. Aycock (below, left), and Furnifold Simmons (below, right)—used fear to drive African Americans from the polls. They brought in South Carolina's Senator "Pitchfork" Ben Tillman to instruct local Democratic clubs on the finer points of terrorism, and Daniels's News and Observer *manufactured and circulated stories of "unspeakable outrages" committed by African American men on white women. Photographs courtesy of the North Carolina Collection, Wilson Library, the University of North Carolina at Chapel Hill.*

And one thing more my song does lack.
I forgot to say the men were black.
Her friends and neighbors will say the same,
And Emma Hartsell was her name.

In "The Death of Emma Hartsell" and several other southern lynching ballads about murdered girls, the victims don't beg for their lives; in fact, they don't speak at all. Emma Hartsell never figures as a full-fledged character in her eponymous ballad because the song's central story is not really about her. The crucial scene in "The Death of Emma Hartsell" is when Joe Kizer begs for a drink of water and is refused. In an important way, the mob in a lynching ballad usurps the power of judgment that is rightly reserved to God. When Joe Kizer begs for water, the man doesn't just deny him water, he condemns him: "To Hell, to Hell your soul must fly." Verse eight spells this out explicitly: Emma goes to heaven, Tom and Joe go to Hell. Nothing in "The Death of Emma Hartsell" suggests that the mob or the ballad's audiences had any doubts about playing judge, jury, executioner, and God with the lives and souls of two black men in 1898. But just eight years later, a poet crafting a ballad about another lynching in a nearby county would turn this judgment on its head, using religion to condemn the lynching.

In 1905 J. V. Johnson was a white farmer living near the Pee Dee River and the South Carolina state line in Anson County, North Carolina. He had a drinking problem and never got along with his in-laws, the wealthiest landowners in the area. One December afternoon, he finished off a running argument with his younger brother-in-law, Guinn Johnson, with both barrels of a shotgun. He telephoned the sheriff and turned himself in, spending the next few months at the Wadesboro jail. After a first trial ended with a hung jury, a mob led by the dead man's brother broke Johnson out of jail on May 31, 1906, and hanged him from a pine tree on the edge of town.

Plyde Marsh, a Wadesboro merchant who had lived near Johnson for a few years, thought the lynching was worth preserving in song. He took the same melody used for "The Death of Emma Hartsell," changed it slightly, and created this ballad:

"J. V. JOHNSON"

'Twas on a gloomy Sunday night
When Johnson thought he was alright,
A hundred hearts of an angry mob
Did disobey the laws of God.

'Twas on land at half past two.
The great steel doors the men broke through.
They scarcely waited for this poor man.
The cell was opened at their command.

Into the cell they boldly went,
And only there a moment spent.

"Come out, come out, your time has come
When you'll repay the deed you've done."

"Don't hurt me boys," he sadly said.
"Hush, hush your mouth—you'll soon be dead."
"Oh, just give me one moment to pray,
And do not kill a man who prays."

"You did not give Guinn time to pray.
You took his dear sweet life away.
We will not give you time to pray,
But for his life your life shall pay."

That was a sad and awful time.
Just as they reached the fatal pine,
A rope around his neck they tied
And hung the man until he died.

"I know the crime is awful black.
I wish that I could call it back.
It is so dark I cannot see.
My soul, what will become of thee?

"Farewell, this world, my friends, my wife.
This mob will surely take my life.
It is so dark I cannot see.
My soul, what will become of thee?"

The contrast between "J. V. Johnson" and "The Death of Emma Hartsell"
could not be sharper. In 1898, when Joe Kizer and Tom Johnson were lynched,
mobs were instrumental in setting up white supremacy in North Carolina; by
1906 the system was well in place and the mob had become more of a problem
than its target for the white-supremacist constituency that it served. Too many
unruly whites might scare off industry and tarnish the reputation of the state. The
mob that lynched J. V. Johnson became the first people prosecuted for lynching
in North Carolina. Although the North Carolina justice system of 1906 would
have been far more inclined to prosecute the mob that lynched Johnson because
he was white than if he had been black, it is a mark of progress that later that summer, two members of a mob were convicted of lynching three African Americans
in Salisbury, north of Charlotte. In "J. V. Johnson," the doomed man speaks and
even gets the last word. Most significantly, beginning with the very first verse,
Marsh used religion to condemn the mob and their actions, not the person the
mob was killing, as is the case with Emma Hartsell's ballad.

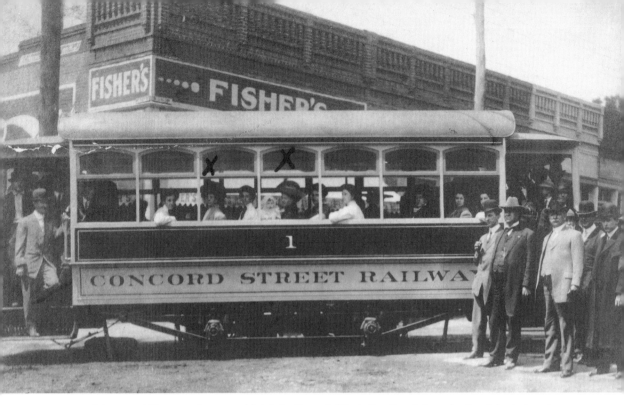

Johnson and Kizer were incarcerated briefly in Concord, North Carolina, before a lynch mob broke into the jail and took them to Big Cold Water Hill outside of town. Turn-of-the-century downtown Concord, courtesy of the North Carolina Collection, Wilson Library, the University of North Carolina at Chapel Hill.

TRACKING THE FORGOTTEN BALLAD

Folklorists usually document traditions that are vigorously alive or perhaps still persisting but in decline. When I was studying these ballads in the mid-1990s at the University of North Carolina, they had all vanished and only one or two people could recall even a fragment of any of them. Folklorist Daniel W. Patterson showed me a transcription of the ballad of J. V. Johnson that a student had recorded thirty years ago. A couple of days in the library led me to a newspaper account of the events the song was based on. Patterson's former student put me in touch with a few people in Anson County, and I slowly began to learn more about the lynching. Looking for more information, I drove down to Wadesboro to spend a day in the library reading through the files of the local newspaper. The murder of Guinn Johnson and the lynching of J. V. Johnson were the biggest news Anson County saw in 1906, and articles spun out the story for weeks. Down the street, I dragged dusty books off the courthouse shelves to piece together the story of how J. V. Johnson came to such an unhappy end. A few weeks later, I got in touch with Eddie Gathings, the retired postmaster of Wadesboro. His father had been living in a room upstairs in one of the buildings downtown when the lynching happened. He heard the crowd outside and even went down to the street and tried to convince them not to kill Johnson. Later, when the sheriff asked him if he had recognized anyone in the mob, he said it was dark and he couldn't be sure. Gathings and I walked through the downtown where the jail used to be and down the streets J. V. Johnson was dragged along ninety years before. Gathings showed me the place where the pine tree, Johnson's Pine, people called it, stood until a few years ago when it was cut down to make way for some new houses. I never did find another soul who knew the ballad, though. Its strong critique of lynching seems to have given "J. V. Johnson" a rather short shelf-life in the oral tradition of the twentieth-century South. "J. V. Johnson" came from a historical moment that saw the beginning of the end of lynching in North Carolina. The disappearance of the song from tradition, though, suggests that songs like "The Death of Emma Hartsell" were what most whites wanted to hear. The subsequent history of Emma Hartsell's ballad underscores this point.

Tracking down information about "The Death of Emma Hartsell" was a little easier, since it seems to have been popular for a much longer time. Once again, I started in the library and wound up in the field, driving around Cabarrus County with notebook, tape recorder, and camera. Thinking back, I was remarkably fortunate to have found some of the people I did, considering that the events I was studying had occurred almost a century before. My first stop once again was the local history room of the county library. A 1934 newspaper article had included both the text of the ballad and an account of the murder of Emma Hartsell. The columnist who wrote that piece still lived in the same town and helped me quite a bit. A newspaper article from the 1960s said that the house where the murder occurred was still standing alongside North Carolina Highway 49, so I went looking for it out of curiosity. I used to drive Highway 49 a lot, and I thought I recognized the building in the old newspaper photograph. It was a little eerie to realize I had driven dozens of times right past the place where Emma Hartsell was killed and never knew it. When I stopped to ask directions that afternoon, I met the son of the doctor who had examined Emma's body, and he gave me stories about the murder and lynching that I had not heard elsewhere. I even corresponded with one of Emma Hartsell's half-brothers and interviewed another. There's more of the past around us than we often realize.

Emma Hartsell's ballad was easier to track down than J. V. Johnson's in part because the story and the ballad had never dropped out of local tradition. One person who sang "The Death of Emma Hartsell" for quite a while was hillbilly music star J. E. Mainer. Born just a few months after Hartsell's death, Mainer had left the mountains and come down to work in the textile mills of Concord in 1922. A fiddler and singer, Mainer soon assembled a band in the rich musical ferment of the textile world, and Mainer's Mountaineers began playing shows and making records. By the mid-1960s country music had left string bands like Mainer's behind, but a new generation of fans was rediscovering the music.

Mainer and the latest incarnation of his band continued to perform around Concord and make records. In the mid-1960s, Mainer became the first person to record "The Death of Emma Hartsell." In about 1967 he published a songbook with some of his better-known songs. Included was "Song of Emma Hartsell," which Mainer claimed to have written in 1966. Anyone ordering the record would receive along with it a copy of the photograph that went with the ballad: two young black men hanging from a tree.

This record and the context in which it was produced are as useful a document of social history as the original ballad. Like the ballad itself, it assumes that Tom and Joe were guilty: as a note to the song said, "Crime doesn't pay." More than that, it assumes that in 1967 there were people interested in hearing a song about the lynching of two black men. Mainer had been a successful musician for too long to misapprehend the tastes of his audience. Just as the song had been created at a time when many whites were learning to be afraid of African American men in public life and politics, the recording of "The Death of Emma Hartsell" appeared at a moment when, in the wake of the Voting Rights Act of 1965, black men and women were finally reemerging as a political force on a large scale. Like the song's original creators, Mainer and his audience reached for a familiar cultural form to address a contemporary issue.

Yet "The Death of Emma Hartsell" had never told the true story of what hap-

In "J. V. Johnson," the doomed man speaks and even gets the last word. In this, he is like another North Carolinian portrayed sympathetically in a ballad before being hanged: Frankie Silver, the only woman hanged by the state of North Carolina. Photograph courtesy of www.frankiesilver.com.

pened in 1898. It was part of a mythology used to create and justify a system of white supremacy. The song said nothing about political agendas or abstract discussions of who should and should not participate in public life in the South. Instead, it presented a simple and clear image: the black beast rapist preying on a helpless white girl and suffering a terrible penalty at the hands of a righteous white mob. For decades, whites heard that ballad and that version of the lynching. Conflicting details in stories about the lynching gradually disappeared until the ballad's version of history was believed. The song that had started out to reflect a social reality had, in time, helped to create it.

books

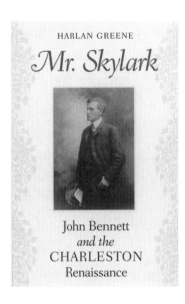

HARLAN GREENE

Mr. Skylark

John Bennett
and the
CHARLESTON
Renaissance

Mr. Skylark

John Bennett and the Charleston Renaissance
By Harlan Greene
University of Georgia Press, 2001
372 pp. Cloth $34.95

Reviewed by **Dale Volberg Reed**, coauthor of *1001 Things Everyone Should Know About the South*, published by Doubleday in 1996.

Harlan Greene has set out to establish that John Bennett was a leading figure in the "Charleston Renaissance," and he brings impressive credentials and a missionary zeal to the project. Greene, a Charlestonian, novelist, and archivist, became fascinated with Bennett while cataloging thirty linear feet of his papers at the South Carolina Historical Society. It's easy to see why.

Bennett was born in 1865, the son of a merchant in Chillicothe, Ohio. During several years of ill health as a child he read and drew avidly, and mastered the art of cutting silhouettes. Dropping out of high school, he worked for a newspaper, then went to Cincinnati to prepare for art school in New York until family business reverses forced him to return to newspaper work. Desperate to go to art school, he freelanced articles, stories, poems, illustrations, and silhouettes, and took any other odd jobs he could find. During these lean years, he developed depression, eyestrain, and allergies, which he treated with patent medicines laced with cocaine, becoming addicted. He recovered, and in 1891 sold his first piece to the *St. Nicholas Magazine* for children. He became a regular contributor, but a bout with cholera brought a return to depression and cocaine. He began going to Salt Sulphur Springs, West Virginia, to rest and recuperate. There he met the Augustine Smythe family, from Charleston, sold them a couple of watercolors, and began a correspondence with Augustine.

In 1895 his struggle began to pay off. He published a great deal, including a poem that was widely reprinted, and later anthologized and set to music (ending up in Bartlett's *Familiar Quotations*). When his sister suggested a story about child actors in Elizabethan England, Bennett wrote *Master Skylark*, a children's book about a boy kidnapped and taken to London in a company of players. *St. Nicholas* bought the serial rights, and Greene used the money to enroll in the Art Students' League in New York. When *Master Skylark* became a bestseller, Bennett tried to follow up his success, even dropping out of art school to write. But his health failed again and he returned to cocaine. When his doctor suggested a warm climate, he accepted Augustine Smythe's invitation to come to Charleston.

There he finished *Barnaby Lee*, which *St. Nicholas* also bought. The money allowed him to marry Susan Smythe in 1902. His marriage into one of Charleston's best families gave him immediate, if tentative, acceptance in Charleston society. He became active in the town's cultural life, assembling a souvenir calendar for the United Daughters of the Confederacy, lecturing to the Federation of Women's Clubs on "Spiritual Songs of the Old Plantations," and beginning to write on Charleston subjects — even began using Gullah dialect in his stories. He was made an honorary curator of the Charleston Museum.

But social disaster loomed. Although he had been in Charleston for a decade, he had not learned what should not be said in front of ladies. In February 1908, he lectured again to the Women's Clubs, this time on "Grotesque Legends of Charleston," using black folktales he had collected. His stories included miscegenation and the word "chemise," and were called by the Charleston *News and Courier* "a startlingly realistic exposition of Revolting Savage Fancies." Charleston society cut him dead, and he began again the cycle of illness, depression, and addiction. He could not write. He retreated to a Smythe estate in North Carolina, where he worked outdoors.

World War I marked the beginning of Charleston's cultural renaissance and the end of Bennett's isolation, as he began to reenter society through volunteer work. The Sketch Club, founded in 1915, was the first of many organizations that revitalized Charleston's cultural life, looking both inward for subject matter and outward to connect with the most up-to-date artists and writers elsewhere. Nationally recognized artists began wintering in Charleston and were welcomed as active members of the community. Artists were among the first to realize the precarious state of Charleston's architecture, and many of them were involved in founding the nation's first preservation society, in 1920. That same year, John Bennett helped to found the Poetry Society, which brought in a string of distinguished visitors including Carl Sandburg, Padraic Colum, Amy Lowell, Gertrude Stein, Donald Davidson, Robert Frost, John Crowe Ransom, Vachel Lindsay, Louis Untermeyer, Stephen Vincent Benet, and Harriet Monroe.

The city was soon filled with cultural groups that fed on each other's energy. The community was relatively small, so amateurs were welcomed. Two other organizations were founded in 1923: the Society for the Preservation of Spirituals and the Etchers' Club. (Bennett's only etching, done as a member of the club, has given him a place in studies of Charleston's art.)

What was Bennett's place in all this delightful ferment? Greene stakes five claims for Bennett, calling him "an author of at least one children's classic, a trail-blazer in the study of Gullah, the language of the coastal South Carolina blacks, an oral historian who had saved black folklore from vanishing, a promoter of talent the likes of DuBose Heyward and Hervey Allen, and a man integral to many cultural movements that had left their stamp on the country and the city." Some of those claims are indisputable, but others are at least exaggerations.

There is no question about the first. Although *Barnaby Lee* seems to have disappeared, *Master Skylark* has never gone out of print. It has been dramatized countless times and is still read and performed. It was on *McCall's Magazine*'s 1956 list of the "100 Best Books of All Time" and a 1984 list of "Forty Books All Students under Sixteen Should Have Read," from a survey by the National Endowment for the Humanities. Bennett's *The Pigtail of Ah Lee Ben Loo*, runner-up for the Newbery Award in 1929, has not fared so well, though the silhouettes with which it is illustrated have not lost their charm.

Was Bennett a "trailblazer in the study of Gullah"? Well, he did publish a long two-part article on Gullah in the *South Atlantic Quarterly* in 1908 and 1909 that may have been the most thorough treatment of the dialect to date, with many fascinating examples and flashes of real scholarship. But, even though writers should not be judged by anachronistic criteria, it is hard to praise. Bennett described Gullah as "only a remnant…of Dorset and Devon; only common English," "a grotesque patois" formed "by ignorance, by indolence, and by a constant dissolution of language," by "laziness, physical and mental." He grudgingly admitted that it contained some African survivals, and that it deserved study, but it is difficult to see what trail he was blazing when as late as 1922 he described Gullah as an "outlandish quacking jargon."

Did Bennett save black folklore from vanishing? He certainly saved *some*, but his was a late and minor contribution to the effort, and Greene's overstatement here is unfortunately typical. As in his writing on language, Bennett's impulse seems to have been more that of a local color writer than a scholar. Greene accepts Bennett's own claim to be "the pioneer in the discovery of the Negro as subject for Southern literature," and even describes him as "always ahead of his time" in treating black life realistically, but Bennett's stories based on Gullah folklore smack more of the nineteenth century than the twentieth, and a 1922 piece in *The Reviewer* seems the worst kind of Victorian exoticism for its own sake.

Greene is on more solid ground when he notes Bennett's importance as a mentor to DuBose Heyward and Hervey Allen. For two years the three met weekly to discuss writing and their work. Bennett paid the younger men the compliment of taking them seriously. But that relationship may have been even more important for Bennett than for his protégés. Although he was supremely confident about "that keen swift instrument, my mind," it had failed him in his confrontation with the supremely assured Charleston elite, and he had always felt insecure about his lack of formal education. He must have relished being honored as an experienced, successful writer—"a master of his craft," as he described himself in 1917. Being needed, however, encouraged one of Bennett's worst habits: he welcomed the excuse to put aside work that was not going well anyway. He had published almost nothing since the disastrous lecture, but as Heyward and Allen helped less and less with the Poetry Society (Heyward's idea, originally), it came to dominate Bennett's life.

All those papers in the archives are both a blessing and a curse for Greene and his readers. While it is lovely to have so much raw material, the problem is that it is not really raw. Bennett felt misunderstood and unappreciated, and set out to be sure the world saw him as he should be seen. Greene does try to distance himself, but is a little too willing to let Bennett decide his own place in history. Usually it is simply a matter of overemphasizing Bennett's influence. For example, Greene is quite sure that Bennett began Charleston's literary renaissance, which, he believes, set off the larger southern renaissance. (But he can't decide when. He says that a Bennett poem of 1911 "would usher in the Charleston Literary Renaissance," but also says that when Bennett was working on *Madame Margot* in 1919, "it was the Charleston literary renaissance he was beginning." At least *Madame Margot*, unlike the poem, deals with a Charleston subject.)

Distance, objectivity, dislike, admiration—it is always a challenge for a biographer to find the right tone. My complaint is not that Greene admires Bennett but that he is too eager to tell the reader what to think. In the end, he simply does not establish that Bennett was essential to the Charleston Renaissance, that he was "the one who had a finger in all these different movements, who observed it from both inside and out simultaneously, and who recorded it with some objectivity."

The book has other problems. The chronology is often confusing, and many careless errors should have been caught by an editor. More recognition of what was going on elsewhere in the South would have been useful, especially in light of Greene's pronouncements about Charleston's relative importance. One also wonders what Heyward and Allen thought about Bennett, since he had so much to say about them.

But even if Bennett is not quite the major figure Greene wants him to be, he is an interesting character who moved in interesting circles, and Greene will undoubtedly remain our best authority on his life. Read casually, this book will give a great deal of pleasure; read critically, it will force the reader to think long and hard about the Southern Renaissance and Charleston's place in it. It is a useful addition to the growing literature on the Charleston Renaissance, best read along with *The Charleston Renaissance* by Martha Severens, Boyd Saunders on Alfred Hutty, Susan Williams on Julia Peterkin, Jim Hutchisson on DuBose Heyward, and the other books on Charleston figures that seem to be coming out every day.

Greene himself will soon contribute further to that literature with his forthcoming work, *Renaissance in Charleston: Art and Life in a Southern City, 1900–1940*, coauthored with Jim Hutchisson.

··

Out Under the Sky of the Great Smokies

A Personal Journal
By Harvey Broome
University of Tennessee Press, 2001
328 pp. Paper $15.95

Reviewed by **Daniel S. Pierce**, assistant professor of history at the University of North Carolina at Asheville and author of *The Great Smokies: From Natural Habitat to National Park*, published by the University of Tennessee Press in 2000.

Characterized by imported garbage and nuclear waste; beer cans and other litter on the side of the road; soil erosion; kudzu growing over abandoned, rusting cars and washing machines; soil contaminated by the use and abuse of chemical fertilizers and pesticides; and sites of massive environmental degradation such as Tennessee's Great Copper Basin—the South's environmental record has been often less than sterling. Harvey Broome, however, is a native southern environmental hero, instead of a villain, and his book *Out Under the Sky of the Great Smokies* extols the glories of nature, rather than chronicling its degradation.

Harvey Broome was a native Knoxvillian, his ancestors some of the earliest European inhabitants of east Tennessee. A lawyer by training, his true calling was as a pioneer environmentalist and lover of nature—particularly the Great Smoky Mountains. Broome was a founding member of the Wilderness Society, its President from 1951 until his death in 1968, and an active leader in the Smoky Mountains Hiking Club.

In praising fellow pioneer environmentalists Aldo Leopold and Bob Marshall, Broome asserted that "the best conservationists are those who fuse sentiment with knowledge." Although Broome does not share the national reputation of his friends and fellow founders of the Wilderness Society, he definitely meets his own criterion for being one of "the best conservationists." Indeed, Broome artfully combines both sentiment and knowledge in a style reminiscent of Leopold's masterpiece, *A Sand County Almanac*. *Out Under the Sky* is replete with fusions of ecological observation and transcendentalist sentiment: "And thus flowed the current of life. The seeds of the silverbell were converted into squirrel; and squirrels were converted into foxes. Everything edible, from mice and chipmunks to roots and berries and apples, was converted into bear. And bear and his tracks are converted into wonder and adventure for man."

Out Under the Sky is a collection of observations Broome recorded on his numerous hikes into the Great Smoky Mountains and other areas of the southern Appalachian region. These descriptions are arranged chronologically from Broome's first backpacking trip into the Smokies in 1917 to one of his crowning achievements, the "Save Our Smokies" hike in 1966, which helped block the construction of a highway across the western end of the Great Smoky Mountains National Park. In between, the book catalogs a changing landscape as the Great Smokies were transformed from the natural habitat of the logger and the cattleman into the natural habitat of the veery and the winter wren.

Broome takes the reader deep into the Smokies, often off-trail—"trails, though a convenience, were not a necessity"—in all seasons and in all types of weather. Indeed, Broome relished hiking through mist-shrouded old-growth forests, sleeping in the rain or rock-hopping in winter on ice-covered boulders just as much as he reveled "in the feeling of god-like attainment afforded by . . . full views on a warm spring day."

Along with his observations of nature, Broome also offers his views on overpopulation, the human need for wilderness, the conflict between environmental protection and tourism promotion, the importance of the study of ecology, and the need for "leave-no-trace camping." Although many of Broome's aphorisms may seem trite and preachy to the twenty-first century mind, one must remember that he issued them long before they became orthodox. Indeed, one is often astounded at Broome's prescience on environmental issues that were of little concern to most of his contemporaries.

In Harvey Broome and *Out Under the Sky of the Great Smokies*, southerners can lay claim to a pioneer environmentalist and a classic of nature writing. Supreme Court justice William O. Douglas—a frequent hiking companion of Broome's—wrote, "When it came to writing about the outdoors and the wilderness, I always rated him along with Henry Thoreau and John Muir." Originally published in 1975, seven years after his death, by Broome's wife and hiking companion Anne Broome, the book received little exposure outside the immediate area of the Smokies. The University of Tennessee Press has done us all a service by deciding to reissue what author and environmentalist Michael Frome—author of a new foreword for this edition—has termed a "timeless work." *Out Under the Sky* is a book to be savored, pondered upon, read and reread, preferably on a rock in the middle of Ramsey Fork in the Greenbriar section of Broome's beloved Smokies.

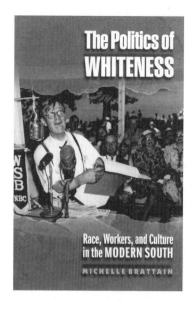

The Politics of Whiteness

Race, Workers, and Culture
in the Modern South
By Michelle Brattain
Princeton University Press, 2001
301 pp. Cloth $35.00

Reviewed by **Carl Burkart**, a doctoral candidate at
the University of Georgia.

For decades, outside observers have wondered why white southern workers in
the twentieth century have so willingly supported demagogues and reactionaries
who offered them nothing but appeals to racial pride. In particular, many have
asked, why did working class southerners follow a couple of decades of support
for New Deal liberalism with a virulent, and sometimes violent, swing to the
right? For most commentators, an unthinking racism blinded whites to their true
economic interests. In *The Politics of Whiteness*, Michelle Brattain challenges this assumption by focusing on the ways that white supremacy brought genuine economic and psychological benefits to cotton mill-hands in Rome, Georgia. Using
union records, newspaper articles, and government documents, Brattain argues
that whiteness, far from being a troublesome distraction, was at the core of the
white worker's place in the South.

In a narrative that is briskly written, closely argued, and generally persuasive,
Brattain follows white mill workers through some of the most volatile periods in
southern politics—from the general strikes of the depression years to wartime
mobilization, postwar labor militancy, and into the Civil Rights era. To unravel
this tangled political thread, she concentrates on white mill workers in a particular place—Rome, Georgia. This community focus allows Brattain to explore differences between firms and even individual workers, and it also allows her to include actors who are often slighted in labor histories. Local newspapermen,
politicians, black activists, and town merchants all play an important part in this
story of working class racial identity.

As *The Politics of Whiteness* moves forward, we learn why so many mill-hands
cheered for Eugene Talmadge, sat out the 1934 General Strike, ignored race baiting, supported the liberal Congress of Industrial Organizations (CIO), crossed
picket lines, and campaigned for George Wallace. The thread that holds these sto-

ries together is Brattain's argument that race, and whiteness in particular, defined wage work for most southerners for historical and structural reasons. As early as the 1880s, industrialists and town boosters justified mill-building campaigns as a way to improve the economic lot of local whites. Thus, wage work, racial solidarity, and company paternalism were interrelated from the beginning. Over the years, the racial make-up of the industrial workforce—the textile industry reserved all non-custodial jobs for white workers—gave race a special economic reality. It also gave white workers a stake in the racial status quo. This intraracial bargain meant more than just not having to compete with African Americans for jobs; it also implied that mill owners had a duty to consider the welfare of the (white) community along with their profit margin. So central was race to southern conceptions of industrial wage work, Brattain maintains, that it often remained, at first glance, implicit.

The whiteness of millwork had an added side effect. During the heyday of the CIO in the 1930s and 1940s, white workers were able to ignore management attempts at race baiting during battles over unionization. They knew that in an all white industry, an organized workforce was likely to protect white jobs. "Race mixing" was simply not an issue. In the years that followed, the organization of even a few mills produced surprising results. Even in a region replete with desperate poverty, intransigent mill owners, and hostile judges, unions were able to transfer their gains in the workplace to the political realm. Indeed, one of Brattain's biggest contributions is her discovery that even politicians who castigated "Big Labor" on the stump were willing to quietly pull strings, pressure judges, and call in favors to help what was, after all, an organized bloc of voters. In this instance, at least, the Georgia Democratic party was expansive enough to include a liberal organization, even if this inclusion was often covert.

In short, Brattain argues that white workers had a big investment in Jim Crow. No wonder federal efforts to integrate schools and workplaces met with hardline opposition from white mill-hands. To make matters worse, even as it was attempting to eradicate white workers' racial privileges, the federal government proved unable to enforce its own labor laws, allowing management to stall and evade National Labor Relations Board decisions. To many in the mill villages, liberalism must have seemed a bad bet. Sadly, Brattain concludes, workers were right. The paternalistic concern and job security of whiteness was the best deal the mill-hands were likely to get. It is no wonder that with the decline of segregation many workers adopted the rhetoric of their better-off neighbors, ignoring the legacy of racism by arguing that blacks got the worst jobs because they were not "qualified" for anything better. It is this rhetoric that we are left with today.

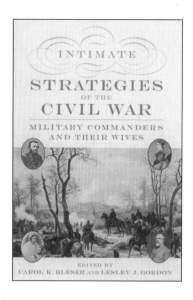

Intimate Strategies
of the Civil War

Military Commanders and Their Wives
Edited by Carol K. Bleser
and Lesley J. Gordon
Oxford University Press, 2001
292 pp. Cloth $30.00

Reviewed by **Nina Silber**, associate professor of
history at Boston University and author of *The Romance
of Reunion: Northerners and the South, 1865–1900*, published
by the University of North Carolina Press in 1993.

Did the spouses of Civil War leaders ultimately affect the outcome of this pivotal
event in American history? Would the war have gone differently if Stonewall
Jackson or William Sherman had listened more to their wives? These are some of
the questions considered in *Intimate Strategies of the Civil War*, although they're not
questions that yield many new revelations. In fact, most authors acknowledge that
wifely influence on wartime strategies was relatively insignificant. And, while
Emory Thomas does hypothesize that Robert E. Lee might never have fought for
the Confederacy were it not for the strong southern sympathies of his wife, Mary,
this portrayal of the unflinching Marse Robert is a little hard to swallow. The same
is true of Jackson, Sherman, Grant, and most of the other eight commanders examined here. A more compelling question, which the essayists also consider, is
this: if the marriages of Civil War leaders did not greatly affect the progress of the
war, how did the war affect those marriages? Looked at from this perspective, *Intimate Strategies of the Civil War* yields some interesting insights—and some exas-
perating misperceptions and missed opportunities.

The book's goal is a promising one: to bridge "the artificial gap separating military history from women and gender studies." Yet, in some ways, the marriages
discussed may not provide the best means for connecting that false divide. The
twelve essays in this collection examine six Confederate and six Union marriages,
and in nearly all cases the husbands were prominent members of society and the
military hierarchy. This meant that some, such as the Confederacy's "first couple," Jefferson and Varina Davis, did not have to endure the prolonged separa-
tions that war often imposes on couples. For others, wealth and family support
insulated wives from many of the more trying repercussions of war. Perhaps not
surprisingly, then, this collection of essays gives us a far more supportive group
of female Confederates than recent scholarship on more ordinary southern

women has suggested. The wives of the top military and political leaders of the South hardly seem a representative bunch on which to base generalizations about the pro- or anti-war sentiments of southern white women.

Of course, even among these elite couples, marriages were tested by the North-South conflict. But marriage is a difficult thing to grasp because so much depends on the complicated melding of individual personalities—something that Civil War Americans struggled with just as much as their twenty-first century descendants. In this regard, *Intimate Strategies* offers greater insight into the ways individual men and women were changed by the war than into how the war specifically altered men and women's marital relations. What stands out most in that light is the enhanced, if often qualified, independence of Civil War wives. In numerous instances, the war prompted married women to take on increased responsibilities and more overtly political roles. Jessie Fremont's insistent protests to Abraham Lincoln on behalf of her husband's emancipation policies in Missouri present the most obvious example of women's wartime politicking. Joshua Chamberlain's wife, Fannie, traveled frequently on her own during her husband's long absences from home; naval commander Phillips Lee's wife, Elizabeth, became the director of an orphan asylum. Even southern wives acquired a semi-independent voice, often following their husband's death. As widows, Varina Davis, Anna Jackson, and LaSalle Pickett all became writers, although, ironically, their writing helped them recreate themselves not as fully autonomous individuals but as professional widows of the Confederacy.

Perhaps the most frustrating feature of this book is its lack of attention to what was undoubtedly a critical influence on southern gender and marital relations: slavery. Surprisingly, the most sustained discussion of "the peculiar institution" comes in John Simon's insightful account of the Grant marriage and the public relations problem posed by Julia's ownership of human property. How can we really understand southern marriage and the Civil War without examining how responsibility for slave management must have shifted (or not) in the course of the conflict, or how couples responded to the breakdown of the institution that had so shaped the identities of southern white slaveowners, women as well as men? Certainly this was something that made Confederate marriages unique. Unfortunately, while this collection helps to remove one artificial gap—between homefront and battlefront—it promotes another unhelpful separation in its segregation of Confederate marriages from southern slavery.

Faulkner's County

The Historical Roots of Yoknapatawpha
By Don H. Doyle
University of North Carolina Press, 2001
488 pp. Cloth $49.95, paper $24.95

Reviewed by **Linda Wagner-Martin**, Frank Borden Hanes Professor of English at the University of North Carolina at Chapel Hill, and author of several books, including *"Favored Strangers": Gertrude Stein and Her Family*, published by Rutgers University Press in 1995.

William Faulkner's imagination has been the subject of literally hundreds of scholarly essays and books. Since his death in 1962, what people see as the enigma of this great American novelist has prompted biographies, close readings of his fictions, and a range of theoretical treatments of those works that still leave students and scholars puzzled. Who *was* Billy Faulkner, the sometimes modest, sometimes flamboyant, and always driven writer? Working within the postage stamp of his homeplace—Lafayette County, Mississippi—Faulkner claimed his right to be considered one of the most significant novelists of modern times, even as his life itself mandated against his ever attaining such a position. What historian Don H. Doyle provides in his *Faulkner's County: The Historical Roots of Yoknapatawpha* is a kind of scaffolding for any number of interpretations of Faulkner's oeuvre. In always clear prose, Doyle provides a wealth of information that supplements what we already know. Doyle shows how much Faulkner's home county gave the inventive writer, in both its commonplace and unremarkable dailiness and its startling, sometimes macabre, events. Faulkner's county, it becomes clear, was not merely the context for his narratives: it often was the starting point for them.

William Faulkner was the fourth generation of his family to inhabit Lafayette County; the legends of the place were his family's stories. As if he were a part of that tradition too, Doyle begins with the beginning: a description of the way the Chickasaw and Choctaw tribes differentiated themselves, and the way the Chickasaw attained legendary status. From before 1540 through 1830, when Mississippi state law replaced tribal law and caused the devastating removal of the tribes, Doyle recounts the uses of Indians to whites—as providers of furs, allies against foreign invasion, successful farmers and land owners (land held by the tribe rather than individuals), and subjects for Christianization. He interweaves the history of the planter culture, the system of slavery, and poor white attempts at survival (the struggling Sutpen-like land owners). His accounts of life in ante-bellum Mississippi are as fascinating as his narrative of the postwar years—the Civil War itself with the destruction of Oxford; Reconstruction with the Ku Klux Klan, bushwhackers, and political battles between the Democrats and the Republicans; and the downward spiral of poverty that fed forests and game into sawmills, and modest families' hopes into a similar waste. Doyle's considerable accomplishment is recounted modestly; he quotes Faulkner's phrase "a few old mouth-to-mouth tales" (from *Absalom, Absalom!*) to suggest the oral source of much of a people's knowledge about their place and time, and past times.

Doyle admires "Faulkner's continued probing of his people's history" and does his best to give the reader information about the facts and contexts of that history. *Faulkner's County* tells of the importance of the Elizabeth Ragland murder, the reasons for burying the family coin and silver, the story of hiding out in attics to remain free from the Confederate provost marshalls, and why the burial of Toby Tubby occasioned protest. He also describes the way Hoka's "X" gives three white men ownership of Oxford, as well as other historical details that Faulkner wrote into Yoknapatawpha legend. For Doyle's aim, as he states, is "to use Faulkner's fiction to inform my historical interpretation and, to a lesser extent, use the history to illuminate Faulkner's world." This appears to be a task only an historian could undertake, and one only a good—and very literate—historian accomplish.

Faulkner's County also illustrates the case study method of historical writing at its best. The author states that he has attempted to provide "a history of a small but characteristic little piece of the American South, 'a postage stamp of native soil,' Faulkner [and/or Sherwood Anderson] called it." One of the convincing conclusions of Doyle's study is to show how firmly—and crucially—Faulkner and his work remain lynchpins of the study of southern culture. In his complex works, the often-overlooked stories as well as the novels, the authentic South, complete with its usually contradictory elements, can begin to be found, excavated, and questioned. Doyle's task, like Faulkner's, was no simple exploration.

George Henry White

An Even Chance in the Race of Life
By Benjamin R. Justesen
Louisiana State University Press, 2001
471 pp. Cloth $45.00

Reviewed by **John H. Haley**, associate professor
emeritus of history at the University of North Carolina
at Wilmington.

In July 1900, George Henry White allegedly stated, "May God damn North Carolina, the state of my birth." If true, what prompted this comment? In 1896 White attained the highest public office of any African American at the time when he was elected to the United States House of Representatives. As the only African American in Congress, White thought of himself as a national leader and the political spokesman for his race. Conversely, white supremacists in North Carolina saw him as an embarrassment to their state. The violent white supremacy campaign of 1898 allowed the "most vicious element of the white race" to gain control of the state. Jim Crow laws were enacted, disfranchisement of the masses of black voters was almost a certainty, and White believed that his third wife's health was permanently impaired due to the invectives and innuendoes aimed at her during political contests. Simply put, white supremacists had virtually destroyed White's life. His reputation, public esteem, and livelihood were seriously damaged, there were threats on his life, and he was a lame duck Republican congressman who would "not go home again" because he no longer felt able to live like a man in North Carolina.

White's life is a poignant reminder of how institutionalized white supremacy curtailed the opportunities for advancement open to African Americans in North Carolina. Born in Bladen County in 1852, White emerged from relative obscurity to become America's "first black superstar, the political savior of his race." Justesen promises to rescue White from near oblivion by reconstructing his life and presenting a "complete portrait of him to others." The result is an intertwining of two stories that approximates the "life and times" genre: a chronological narrative that attempts to reconstruct White's political career, and an analytical narrative that relates primarily to his character, emotions, motivations, and family and personal relationships. Unfortunately, this narrative is often speculative or it springs mainly from the author's imagination, and, regardless of the extensive notes, the text frequently lacks creditable documentation.

We still know nothing substantive of the formative years of White's life, or the first two decades of his existence—periods that are crucial to biographers' understanding of their subjects. After receiving a normal certificate from Howard University in 1877, he moved to New Bern where he was employed as a school principal. Meanwhile, he read law under William John Clark, and in 1880 he was licensed to practice law. His reputation as a respected prosperous attorney, his membership in a host of civic and fraternal organizations, his charisma, and skill at oratory all enhanced his "natural affinity for politics." Regretfully, Justesen primarily focuses on elite personalities and offers little explanation of White's appeal or his relationship with the masses of voters. Before serving in the United States Congress, White had won election to the North Carolina House of Representatives in 1881, the Senate in 1884, and to the position of Solicitor of the Second Judicial District in 1886 and 1890. As was the case in the General Assembly of North Carolina, White's minority status prevented him from becoming an effective U.S. Congressman. He was important, though, because he gave voice to a wide range of issues of significance to his race. White insisted that African Americans would not be satisfied with anything less than equal treatment under the law, and the removal of all legal barriers erected against them. "An equal chance in the race of life is all we ask." When disfranchisement decimated the ranks of black voters in North Carolina, White and his family moved to Washington, D.C., where he soon discovered that he was expendable to the Republican Party. Unable to secure a government position, White practiced law, invested in a brick manufacturing company, and in 1906 moved to Philadelphia, where he established a savings bank. He also continued to work on the development and promotion of Whitesboro, "an ethnically homogeneous environment for utopian pioneers," in Cape May County, New Jersey. White died in his sleep at the age of sixty-four in January 1919.

George Henry White raises some difficult issues. Part of the book is factual and based on sound historical evidence. Part is concocted, conditional, or speculative. Because White left no personal papers, his voice, motivations, and actions spring mainly from the author's imagination or they are constructed through the lens of others. The narrative is peppered with notes that frequently provide analogies and information—but no documentation. Granted, a certain amount of literary license may be acceptable, but in this case there is a little too much.

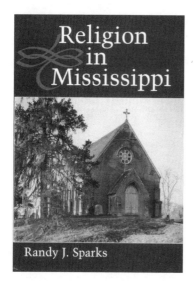

Randy J. Sparks

Religion in Mississippi

By Randy J. Sparks

University Press of Mississippi, 2001

291pp. Cloth $40.00

Reviewed by **David Edwin Harrell Jr.**, Daniel F. Breeden Eminent Scholar in the Humanities at Auburn University and author of *The Churches of Christ in the Twentieth Century: Homer Hailey's Personal Journey of Faith*, published by the University of Alabama Press in 2000.

This sweeping survey of religion in Mississippi provides a guide for viewing the religious experience of the whole South. Randy Sparks has read broadly in the growing body of literature on southern religious history, and he carefully summarizes competing interpretations as he proceeds from colonial Catholicism to the contemporary stresses in mainstream Protestant denominations.

For the most part, Sparks's eleven chapters focus on the two topics that he knows best and that he judges to be most critical: the dominant role of Protestant evangelicalism in the region, and the bedeviling influence of race prejudice. His research in original sources is impressive, and he has an eye for colorful quotes that make for good reading.

Religion in Mississippi incorporates modern religious outsiders such as Catholics, Jews, and Mormons, but the main story is the growth of a Methodist-Baptist-Presbyterian dominance after the American Revolution. These churches won the South as a part of the broader "democratization" of American religion; before 1830, they formed a creative "counterculture" that empowered the common people and played fast and loose with social conventions. Sparks is at his best telling tales of the camp meetings that were, in the words of Methodist Bishop Francis Asbury, the Lord's "battle ax and weapon of war."

While they did not completely level frontier society, early-nineteenth-century evangelicals appealed to all: "Women and slaves were drawn to evangelicalism by the respect, the spiritual equality, and the substantive leadership opportunities that it offered." In an excellent chapter on black religion from 1799 to 1860 Sparks paints a broad picture of interracial meetings, enduring independent and quasi-independent black congregations and preachers, repressive white efforts to control black religion after 1830—in all, a highly complex religious landscape.

Things changed in the South after 1830. Slave revolts and radical abolitionism account for much of that change, but Sparks concentrates on another development that revolutionized southern evangelicalism. "Flush times" separated planters from yeomen farmers; the democratic sects of the early nineteenth century increasingly became formal denominations led by educated clergymen. That was not good news for the equalitarian evangelicals lionized by Sparks: "The period from 1830 to 1860 saw a major shift in evangelical theology as progressives abandoned the traditional evangelical emphasis on the equality of believers and advocated instead a hierarchical, corporate view of the religious community, a change with tremendous implications for blacks and women."

Religion in Mississippi describes an increasingly denominational and domesticated evangelicalism after the Civil War. Evangelicals remained ubiquitous but became more and more divided. Some preachers and women's groups were more responsive to social injustice than generally assumed; Methodist Bishop Charles B. Galloway, for instance, championed women's rights and anti-lynching laws. But mainstream evangelical churches paid a price for even moderate bows to reform and political liberalism; increasingly in the twentieth century they were outflanked by new groups to their right—Pentecostals, churches of Christ, and other conservative churches.

In a chapter on religion and civil rights Sparks returns to the question that most troubles his conscience: how did Mississippi Christians, white and black, evangelicals and outsiders, respond to the moral challenge to combat racial injustice? Not very well, he concludes. It is true that one can point to white liberals who refused to compromise their faith (between 1959 and 1964 seventy-nine Methodist ministers transferred out of the Mississippi Conference) and to "courageous" black leaders, but there were also black ministers "in the pay of whites" and, of course, hard-line Christian segregationists. Still, most Mississippi Christians were probably somewhere in the middle; at the time, historian James W. Silver observed that "almost every congregation in the state was composed of individuals who ranged from liberal to racist." Sparks's treatment adds needed depth to this tragic era. He clearly states the dilemma of the moderate middle, a group that begs further study: "Attacked by right-wing segregationists for being too liberal and almost equally denounced by their coreligionists outside the region for being too conservative, white religious leaders across the state were virtually paralyzed."

For his part, Sparks has little sympathy for the weak and faint-hearted who so transparently bent to conform: "In most respects, churches as institutions, whether black of white, failed to exert courageous leadership on civil rights until forced by their members or compelled by events to do so." Evangelicalism began as a powerful democratic surge among frontiersmen who came dangerously close to actually believing that everyone was equal in Christ. Regrettably, Sparks thinks, they got over it as they became better educated, more affluent, and learned good manners. With regard to the central moral dilemma faced by southern evangelicals, they were weighted in the balance and found wanting. Sparks gives us some reason to believe that Mississippi evangelicals were better men and women than the worst of the sinners who surrounded them, but, alas, they proved to be in the world and of it.

There is nothing stunningly new in this book; it is a survey that moves chronologically from period to period in a predictable pattern. But it does so clearly and often with a genuine feel for the people who lived the South's religious experience. The author's moral sensibilities provide a high bar for measuring his subjects; he fervently wishes they had done better, but, kindly, he assigns only a few irrevocably to hell.

About the Contributors

Bruce E. Baker is a doctoral student in history at the University of North Carolina at Chapel Hill. His essay "North Carolina Lynching Ballads" appeared in *Under Sentence of Death: Lynching in the South*, a collection edited by W. Fitzhugh Brundage, and he currently is studying the historical memory of Reconstruction in the South during the twentieth century.

Philip Beidler is professor of English at the University of Alabama, where he has taught American literature since receiving his Ph.D. from the University of Virginia. His recent books include *The Good War's Greatest Hits: World War II and American Remembering,* and *First Books: The Printed Word and Cultural Formation in Early Alabama.*

Julian Bond is Chairman of the Board of the NAACP and a professor of history at the University of Virginia. He was a founder of the Student Nonviolent Coordinating Committee in 1960, and he served for more than twenty years in the Georgia General Assembly.

Lynn A. Casmier-Paz is assistant professor of English at the University of Central Florida. She writes on race, literacy, slave narratives, and autobiography studies, and has just completed an article titled "Slave Narratives and the Rhetoric of Author Portraiture," which will appear in *New Literary History.*

Charlie Curtis has worked in photography and estate gardening, and lives in Free Union,

Virginia, with his wife, Jackie, and his daughter, Emily. In addition to publishing his photographs in magazines, he currently is working to bring his pictures together in book form.

John Shelton Reed, who recently retired from university life, was the William Rand Kenan Jr. Professor of Sociology and the director of the Odum Institute for Research in Social Science at the University of North Carolina at Chapel Hill. Among his recent books is *1001 Things Everyone Should Know About the South*, written with his wife, Dale Volberg Reed. He is coeditor of *Southern Cultures.*

Anne Firor Scott is W. K. Boyd Professor of History Emerita at Duke University and a pioneer in the study of southern women's history. Her book *The Southern Lady: From Pedestal to Politics, 1830–1930* has been constantly in print since its publication in 1970.

James Seay is professor of English at the University of North Carolina at Chapel Hill and the author of four books of poetry.

Harry L. Watson is professor of history at the University of North Carolina at Chapel Hill and director of UNC's Center for the Study of the American South. His publications include *Liberty and Power: The Politics of Jacksonian America*, published by Hill & Wang. He also is coeditor of *Southern Cultures.*

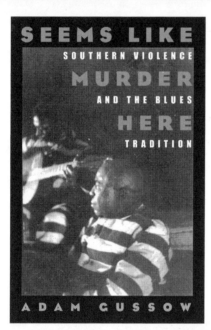

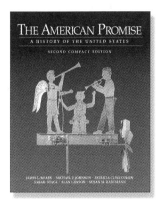
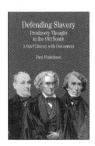
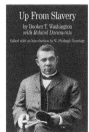

Might as well get *Southern Cultures* the easy way. Subscribe now and save over 35%.

The Southern Movie Palace
Rise, Fall, and Resurrection

Janna Jones

"Jones takes us back to the heyday of the silver screen, when going downtown to an extravagant movie palace was the highlight of the week. Then she shows how contemporary visionaries have preserved and reinterpreted these grand old theaters for a modern 'going downtown' experience."—Thomas Graham, Flagler College, St. Augustine
February. Cloth, $24.95

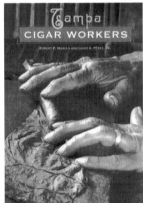

Dixie's Daughters
The United Daughters of the Confederacy and the Preservation of Confederate Culture

Karen L. Cox

"A vital and, until now, missing piece to the puzzle of the 'Lost Cause' ideology and its impact on the daily lives of post-Civil War southerners."—Carol Berkin, City University of New York
New Perspectives on the History of the South. April. Cloth, $55.00

Tampa Cigar Workers
A Pictorial History

Robert P. Ingalls and Louis A. Pérez, Jr.

"Combining powerful images with compelling quotes, Ingalls and Pérez capture the extraordinary world the cigar workers created and the imprint it has left on the historical landscape even after its demise."—Nancy A. Hewitt, Rutgers University
February. Cloth, $29.95

Gendered Freedoms
Race, Rights, and the Politics of Household in the Delta, 1861-1875

Nancy D. Bercaw

"An exciting, important book . . . a significant contribution that recasts our understanding of the terrain of southern history."—Laura E. Edwards, Duke University
Southern Dissent Series
March. Cloth, $55.00

Making Waves
Female Activists in 20th-Century Florida

Edited by Jack E. Davis and Kari Frederickson

"These essays lift up the lives of outstanding Florida women who helped shape the course of 20th-century Florida."—James B. Crooks, University of North Florida
The Florida History and Culture Series
February. Cloth, $55.00

Florida's Farmworkers in the 21st Century

Nano Riley and Davida Johns

"Historically, farmworkers have been among the most exploited of America's many laboring groups. They are not forgotten people, but they are indeed America's most ignored. In a book of significant social importance, Nano Riley and Davida Johns remind us, with honesty and passion, of Florida's own 'harvest of shame'."—Jack Davis, University of Alabama at Birmingham
The Florida History and Culture Series
March. Cloth, $24.95

Order through full-service booksellers, our website at www.upf.com, or with VISA, American Express, or M/C toll free: 1-800-226-3822

Gainesville, Tallahassee, Tampa, Boca Raton, Pensacola, Orlando, Miami, Jacksonville, Fort Myers

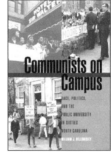

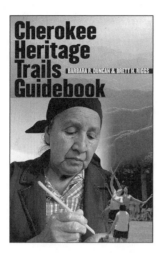